Augsburg College
George Sverdrup Library
Minneapolis, Minnesota 55454

Innovation in Communist Systems

Other Titles in This Series

Hungary: An Economic Geography, György Enyedi

The Future of Agriculture in the Soviet Union and Eastern Europe: The 1976-1980 Five-Year Plans, edited by Roy D. Laird, Joseph Hajda, and Betty A. Laird

The Liberated Female: Life, Work, and Sex in Socialist Hungary, Ivan Volgyes and Nancy Volgyes

Population and Migration Trends in Eastern Europe, edited by Huey Louis Kostanick

A Case Study of a Soviet Republic: The Estonian SSR, edited by Tönu Parming and Elmar Järvesoo

Yugoslavia After Tito: Scenarios and Implications, Gavriel D. Ra'anan

The Soviet Agrarian Debate: A Controversy in Social Science, 1923-1929, Susan Gross Solomon

The German Democratic Republic: A Developed Socialist Society, edited by Lyman H. Legters

Perspectives for Change in Communist Societies, edited by Teresa Rakowska-Harmstone

The Future of the Soviet Economy: 1978-1985, edited by Holland Hunter

Soviet Involvement in the Middle East: Policy Formulation, 1966-1973, Ilana Kass

A Short History of the Hungarian Communist Party, Miklós Molnár

Westview Special Studies on the Soviet Union and Eastern Europe

Innovation in Communist Systems
edited by Andrew Gyorgy and James A. Kuhlman

This work focuses on one of the key problems of modern communism: its seeming inability to effect major political, economic, and technological changes in a given Soviet society. Despite this weakness, powerful forces are at work to bring about a multiplicity of important ideological and technical reforms in the Soviet Union and Eastern Europe. Contributors to this volume examine in detail such challenges to the Soviet Union's and Eastern Europe's political systems as human rights, European security, ethnicity, Western diplomacy, Eurocommunism, ostpolitik, and SALT. They portray graphically both the short- and long-term implications of the concepts of innovation and diffusion in East European political cultures.

Andrew Gyorgy is professor of international affairs and political science at the Institute of Sino-Soviet Studies, George Washington University. He has written and edited several books, most recently *Nationalism in Eastern Europe* and (with Peter Toma and Robert Jordan) *Basic Issues in International Relations*, and has contributed to scholarly books and periodicals.

James A. Kuhlman is professor and chairman of the Department of Government and International Studies at the University of South Carolina. He is author and editor of several books, including *Changes in European Relations* and *The Foreign Policies of Eastern Europe*, and is general editor of the series "Studies in U.S. National Security."

Innovation in Communist Systems
edited by Andrew Gyorgy
and James A. Kuhlman

Westview Press/Boulder, Colorado

*Westview Special Studies on
the Soviet Union and Eastern Europe*

All rights reserved. No part of this publication may be reproduced or transmitted in any form or by any means, electronic or mechanical, including photocopy, recording, or any information storage and retrieval system, without permission in writing from the publisher.

Copyright © 1978 by Westview Press, Inc.

Published in 1978 in the United States of America by
  Westview Press, Inc.
  5500 Central Avenue
  Boulder, Colorado 80301
  Frederick A. Praeger, Publisher

Library of Congress Cataloging in Publication Data
Main entry under title:
Innovation in Communist systems.
  (Westview special studies on the Soviet Union and Eastern Europe)
  "Based upon a workshop conference on the adoption and diffusion of new ideas within the Socialist community, sponsored by the Institute for Sino-Soviet Studies at the George Washington University, Washington, D.C., April 29-30, 1977."
  1. Communist state—Congresses. 2. Communism—Europe, Eastern—Congresses. 3. Communism—Europe—Congresses. 4. Communism—China—Congresses. I. Gyorgy, Andrew, 1917- II. Kuhlman, James A. III. George Washington University, Washington, D.C. Institute for Sino-Soviet Studies.
JC474.I5   320.9'171'7   77-29048
ISBN 0-89158-418-8

Printed and bound in the United States of America

Contents

Introduction, *Andrew Gyorgy and James A. Kuhlman* ..1

Part 1
Changes and Innovative Areas in Political Systems

1. Policy Science as an Innovative Area in
   Socialist Systems, *William A. Welsh* 13
2. Political Groupings and Their Role in the
   Process of Change in Eastern Europe,
   Roger E. Kanet 41
3. Eurocommunism and Innovation: A Western
   European Perspective, *Martin O. Heisler* 59

Part 2
Diffusion of Innovation across Systems

4. Yugoslav Self-Management and Its Influence
   on Other Socialist States, *Gary K. Bertsch* 75
5. Problems Facing the Yugoslav Communist
   Movement: A Comment, *R. V. Burks* 99
6. Two Germanies and the Transformation of
   Europe, *John M. Starrels* 105
7. The Impact of Eurocommunism on the
   Socialist Community, *Joan Barth Urban* 115

Part 3
The International Environment as Innovator

8. U.S. Foreign Policy as an Agent of Change in
   Communism, *Robert S. Wood* 143
9. Internationally Diffused Innovation and
   Conditions of Change in Eastern Europe,
   Arpad Abonyi 163
10. Eastern Europe and Eurocommunism as
    Indicators of Soviet Change, *Peter C. Ludz* 179
11. The Kremlin and Problems of Innovation,
    Dan N. Jacobs 199

List of Contributors 211
Index 215

Innovation in Communist Systems

Introduction

Andrew Gyorgy and James A. Kuhlman

With a handful of notable exceptions in the discipline of political science at large and with even fewer exceptions in the field of comparative communist studies, most of the literature on political processes has two major conceptual focuses—change and constancy.[1] Given the natural political and ideological orientation of Western social science, it is no surprise that communist political systems have usually been described and explained in terms of their intransigence and reluctance to accept change even in the face of insurmountable odds. The most thought-provoking and exciting analyses of socialist systems in recent years have been devoted to the concept of change; where, when, and in what ways have the doctrinal traditions of the past given ground to pressures within and without the bureaucratic organizations and revolutionary belief systems institutionalized in the Soviet Union and Eastern Europe?[2]

In addition to the first two basic categories, namely change and constancy, there is an increasing awareness of a third dimension operational in the dynamic processes of communist countries. This dimension clearly implies a stage at which a qualitative economic and political redirection of past patterns becomes mandatory. In the study of communist systems, therefore, the attention of social scientists is focused on the times and places at which constancy yields to change and, in turn, at which change of a given type yields to major *innovative* reforms with unusual and indeed unexpected social, scientific, and ideological significance.

Based upon a Workshop Conference on the Adoption and Diffusion of New Ideas within the Socialist Community—sponsored by the Institute for Sino-Soviet Studies at The George Washington University, Washington, D.C., April 29-30, 1977—this edited volume brings together several analytical approaches to the study of change in communist systems, on the one hand, and reviews the implications of innovation within the Soviet-East European region, on the other hand. In particular, it spells out the significant directions for future research on the diffusion of innovation in socialist polities.

The adoption of new directions in public policy is almost always a conscious one in centralized, hierarchical systems such as those in the Soviet Union and Eastern Europe. The adoption of innovation is by no means voluntary. Frequently, the adopters of change in communist systems are responding to environmental pressures within and without the communist party organizations and communist party-state national boundaries. Thus not only the adoption of innovation but also the source and means of diffusing that innovation must be known before future patterns of change and innovation can be predicted.

Nowhere is the problem of innovation, its adoption and diffusion, more clearly evident and critical than in the area of economic and technological change. Two exemplary presentations to this conference, not included in these printed proceedings, outlined the context in which the tension between constancy of ideology and system maintenance, on the one hand, has confronted the changing internal conditions and external environment, on the other hand.[3] Professor R. V. Burks emphasized the essential interconnection in the advanced industrial systems of the West between technological innovation and social pluralism, contrasting that phenomenon with the communist, and in particular Soviet, practice of aiming at self-sufficiency and central allocation of resources. The impact of these differential approaches to coping with environmental change—voluntary and competitive processes versus involuntary and command responses—is evident in certain unavoidable concessions, such as in the Soviet campaign for Western investment and technological transfer.

Corresponding with the internal demands for a consumer orientation in the Soviet Union and other East European countries are the external demands of the scientific and technological revolution and the necessary integration with the world market. To what extent communist elites are willing or able to tolerate partial pluralization in the face of such pressures is a fundamental question for the possibilities of innovation in socialist communities. As examples, we have witnessed the Prague Spring and August events in Czechoslovakia.

Professor Joseph S. Berliner, noting that the market concept in capitalist countries goes far beyond its shared purpose with the centralized planning concept in socialist economies, drew particular attention to the function of the market in the promotion of technological change. According to Berliner, Soviet attention was not directed specifically at technological advance. Instead, it emphasized allocation, with the belief that once the energies of the working masses were released, the rate of technological development would be enormously enhanced. But the distributive function of centralized planning has fared much better than the processes of technological advance. Furthermore, Berliner stressed that in fact the basic structural forms of Soviet management have proved to be biased against, not just neutral to, innovation.

In the economic areas of organization, prices, and incentives, Berliner proceeded to point out that the system was invariably geared to resist qualitative change. The area of incentive provides a classic illustration of the general point raised by Berliner. Since the primary obligation of a socialist manager is to fulfill the planned assignment, the system of incentives was so designed. But because innovation increases the risk of underfulfillment of the planned goal, the incentives were in fact prohibitive to innovation. Berliner did note that change in each area was occurring, though unclear and uncharted to date. He specifically pointed out that there are no research and development institutes for political innovations, although in some sense such organizations as the Institute for the Study of the USA and Canada might serve notice in the future as a potential agent for innovation in Soviet elite perceptions of North America. Berliner correctly asserted that technological innovation involves less ideological content than does social innovation, that the costs and benefits of technological innovation are easier to identify and measure than those of social innovation, that the relative importance of voluntary and involuntary innovation may be different in technological as opposed to social innovation, that technological innovation is more easily transmitted across national borders than is social innovation, and that technological innovation is more decisive for attaining economic ends than social innovation is for attaining social ends.

There was some measure of disagreement with Professor Berliner's conclusion about the fruitfulness of studying innovation for the purpose of understanding communist systems. Several contributions in this volume address the complexities of the adoption and diffusion of innovation across time and space. Irrespective of the type of innovation—technological or social—the dimensions of time and space lead one to accept the inevitable significance of the process of change and the specific questions as to when and

Introduction 5

where such change might provoke innovative events and behavior. In fact, these fundamental dimensions of the problem preclude the necessity of treating social and technological innovation as discrete types and point to a direction for research that may identify a correlational, even causal, association between the two types.

The book's three parts—"Changes and Innovative Areas in Political Systems," "Diffusion of Innovation across Systems," and "The International Environment as Innovator"—provide a framework within which the student of communist politics is made aware of key factors influencing Soviet and East European leaders and publics. Particular attention is directed to the problem of differentiating processes that indicate simple change and processes that give clues to actual departure from past practices, or to a redirection of existing patterns. The book raises the fundamental questions about the countries and ways in which we are likely to see real changes in communist political behavior.

Part 1 of the book discusses the problem of studying change in communist countries and analyzes the intrastate impact of groups and political processes on the future of these systems. Sources of change from within the communist system are viewed in the context of modernization and a resulting complexity faced by the communist elites. The scientific community, ethnic and national cultures, and economic interests are shown to be significant sources of potential innovation in the ways leaders reach decisions in socialist systems.

Drawing upon extensive experience in collaborative research with members of the socialist scientific community, Professor William A. Welsh analyzes policy science as an innovative area in socialist systems. By attempting to find the "nexus between science and the development of public policy" in socialist systems, his chapter is of at least heuristic value in demonstrating the interconnection between social and technological innovation. Welsh provides succeeding chapters with alternative definitions of innovation derived from a broad spectrum of social scientific literature. He raises the fundamental point that the meaning of an innovation must be "contextualized" as it occurs across the extremely variegated Eastern European systems. What may be innovative in one area of the region may not be innovative in another area. Where contagious diffusion of innovation may suffice in some cases, hierarchically designed innovation provides the only possible means of diffusion in others.

In his chapter Professor Roger E. Kanet enters the conceptual quagmire of "change," "development," and "modernization"—as contexts within which innovative events and behavior are supposed to occur. The agents of adoption and diffusion addressed in this chapter are "subsystems" and "groupings." Empirical references for these concepts are drawn primarily from Czechoslovakia, the German Democratic Republic (GDR), Hungary, and Poland. In concert with the approach taken by Welsh, Kanet discusses the development and behavior of "groupings" in connection with the process of policymaking and then broadly relates this process to the dynamics of social change. The groupings to which he refers are seen as extending their influence beyond the narrow realm of economics into all aspects of society. Furthermore, he sees the groupings themselves as intimately connected with the internal goals of continued economic growth and with the external objectives of more flexible relations with the Soviet Union and the Western world. Professor Martin O. Heisler stresses the importance of political groups and their impact on the Eurocommunist movement.

Part 2 of the book narrows the focus to specific case studies: the influence of the Yugoslav system, acknowledged to be the most experimental in the region, upon other nations in the socialist community; the special connection between West and East Germany; and the phenomenon of

Eurocommunism. These chapters emphasize the multi-dimensionality of change and the practical implications of innovation for even the most closed and impermeable systems in the Soviet–East European community.

Workers' self-management in Yugoslavia has effected changes in a number of other socioeconomic systems outside East Europe. In fact, the resistance to change in the socialist systems may be measured by the degree to which the Yugoslav experiment has been adopted by distant (non–East European), as opposed to proximate, political elites. Professor Gary K. Bertsch correctly concludes that the diffusion of the workers' self-management experiment into Eastern Europe has not been extensive, much less intensive, in any given location. Again, he indicates that a major reason for this is the "indivisibility of the innovation," in other words, the inevitable relationship among social, technical, economic, and political impacts of innovation. A change toward positive conditions for innovation is tentatively pointed out by Bertsch, namely, the same sort of "more pragmatic" leadership as discussed by Welsh and Kanet.

The paradoxes implicit in extensive and intensive socio-technical and economic change, on the one hand, and politico-ideological constancy, on the other hand, are nowhere more perplexing than in the national and international relationships between the German states. Professor John M. Starrels views the specific flow of influence from West to East in the German context. He points in particular to the East Germans' economic incentive as the quid pro quo for human rights concessions on their part. Whether such conscious adoption of change on the part of East German elites should be classified as innovation is a simple matter of research over time. It would be premature to forecast innovative events and behavior on the part of the German Democratic Republic, but the variety of agents and adopters of change emerging as a result of an increasing interaction with the external environment demands a continual monitoring. Similarly, the special relationship among all European communist parties may be seen as a productive area of research for the diffusion of innovation. There was considerable debate at the conference about the direction of change and diffusion of innovation in the East-West context of Eurocommunism. The paramount paradox in this context may be found in the Soviet refusal, noted by Professor Peter C. Ludz of the University of Munich, to recognize demands by East European allies for more equitable relationships within the region, while at the same time the Soviet system itself has made socioeconomic concessions to global environmental pressures. Professor Joan Barth Urban then emphasizes the moderating influence of Eurocommunists upon the Soviet-East European bloc.

This theme is given further attention in Part 3, which stresses the fact that the socialist community is part of a larger international system, despite significant ideological and substantive differences. The impact of the global economy and the potential influence of the United States are given specific assessment in calculating the probability of innovation under communism. In his chapter on models of change in the East European community, Arpad Abonyi deals with the possibilities of innovation according to the context of levels of analysis. Despite the global phenomenon of regionalism, the internal realities of the Soviet-East European subsystem evidence continuing and clearcut limits within which socioeconomic innovation may encroach upon the constancy of party supremacy.

In the concluding section, Professor Robert S. Wood looks at the specific relationship of the United States and the Soviet Union in terms of the ability to induce innovation. Despite the overt reactions of the Soviets to such foreign policy campaigns as the current U.S. stress on human rights, Wood concludes on a note of pessimism: the international environment will bring little change for communist systems. In sum, these essays' different approaches and different conclusions in no way detract from the significance of the subject. Rather, the various chapters show the need for further research on change, in particular on innovation, in communist countries. The variety of that innovative experience to date is evident in these essays and is sufficient reason to continue the pursuit of knowledge of innovation in communist systems. Professor Dan N. Jacobs summarizes the conference essays in a synthesis that may well strike a balance between traditional assumptions of communist party behavior, i.e., elite and even sometimes one-man control, and more recent interpretations of changing conditions, namely, the growing pluralism in formerly monolithic systems: he concludes that when that one leader becomes primus inter pares, he may seek "to build his reputation and personal machine by introducing new measures to deal with real problems."

As a final note, the editors of this volume must acknowledge the contributions of all conferees, those we are fortunate enough to have in print as well as those whose presence at the deliberations was essential to this final product. Most crucial of all was the support of the Institute for Sino-Soviet Studies of The George Washington University and, in particular, of its director, Dr. Gaston J. Sigur. As originators and editors of these proceedings, we are in debt to all of these colleagues, and we are fully aware that the ultimate evaluation of this collective effort rests in our ability to draw together considerable, although often conflicting, expertise.

Notes

1. Among the notable exceptions are Zvi Gitelman, *The Diffusion of Political Innovation: From Eastern Europe to the Soviet Union* (Beverly Hills, Calif.: Sage Publications, 1972); Joseph Berliner, *Innovation Decision in Soviet Industry* (Cam-

bridge, Mass.: MIT Press, 1976); and Leon Smolinski, "East European Influences on Soviet Economic Thought and Reforms" (Bloomington, Ind.: International Development Research Center, Working Paper no. 6, September 1971).

2. See Chalmers Johnson, ed., *Change in Communist Systems* (Stanford, Calif.: Stanford University Press, 1970).

3. Luncheon remarks on the subject of "Technological and Social Innovation" by Joseph H. Berliner of Brandeis University and a dinner address entitled "Innovation under Communism" by R. V. Burks of Wayne State University.

Part 1
Changes and Innovative Areas in Political Systems

1. Policy Science as an Innovative Area in Socialist Systems

William A. Welsh

Innovation and Diffusion in Public Policy Studies

Most of us participating in this conference would consider ourselves social scientists. One of our obligations as such, when we begin to use terminology that is new in our areas of interest, is to connect our usage as explicitly as we can with work that has already been done by others who have used the same concepts. Similarly, the more explicit we can be about the way in which we use critical terms, the more likely we will communicate effectively and avoid the common and distracting confusion of substantive with semantic questions. With that in hand, I would like briefly to call attention to the substantial body of literature that deals with innovation.[1] Elsewhere, a colleague and I have reviewed some of the theoretical literature on innovation and related concepts, especially with an eye to applying it to methodological issues that are important in political science.[2]

It should be kept in mind that innovation is not synonymous with change. The latter is a broader concept; innovation is a special kind of change. It is reasonable to assume that the organizers of this conference have used the term *innovation* consciously and that they mean for us to attempt to identify those changes in policy in socialist systems that are genuinely innovative in character. No purpose would be served by trying to impose any particular definition of innovation on our discussions—and any such effort would probably fail—but it does seem worth urging that we each define terms such as *innovation* or *change* as clearly as we can so that we will know what we are talking about.

The theoretical literature on diffusion and innovation, much of which has been generated by anthropologists, rural sociologists, geographers, and communication theorists, implies the importance of raising certain questions about the concept of innovation as applied to matters of public policy. One question is whether innovation is basically a threshold concept or a step-function concept. Figure 1 sketches three distinct notions of innovation, the first of which is a threshold conception, the second of which is a level-dependent (more restrictive) step-function conception, and the third of which is a level-independent (and therefore broader) step-function conception.

When we use a threshold conception of innovation, we are saying that innovation is defined in terms of the absolute magnitude of change away from some base line level. When the extent of change reaches some (subjectively defined) level—no matter what the shape of the curve describing the change process, and no matter how long the change has been under way—we say that an innovation has taken place. Thus, a threshold conception would accept the possibility that the cumulative impact of incremental change might be innovative. This is represented by case A in Figure 1.

Step-function conceptions of innovation suggest that it is not so much the level of presence of a new practice that is important. Rather it is the change in the slope, statistically speaking; that is, a change in the rate of change itself or, more loosely and descriptively put, a qualitative redirection of policy. In the case of level-dependent step-function definitions (case B in Figure 1), we stipulate that whether a given change is to be treated as "innovative" depends on the value of the change variable itself or of some other relevant variable. For example, the conditional variable might be some measure of industrial development; certain technological changes in modes of production might be considered innovative in economies below a critical level of industrialization, but not considered innovative in more advanced economies. When step-function definitions are not made level-dependent (case C in Figure 1), the change in the slope of the trend line alone is decisive; there is no conditional level to be considered.

The issue is not merely semantic. Everything we know about social, economic, and political change suggests that the processes that characterize incremental change are distinctly different from those that characterize "qualitative," or step-function changes. It is rather fascinating, I think, to attempt to list some of the most important "innovations" that have taken place in socialist systems in the last, say, twenty years according to one type of definition or the other. Thus economic reforms (the new economic mechanisms), changes in methods of elite succession and replacement, and perhaps a renewed emphasis in military strategy on conventional means of warfare might be viewed as step-function innovations. By contrast, a growing inclination toward peaceful coexistence and a less competitive posture politically toward the West, the remission of terror as a control agent, and the increasing use of professional co-optation as an elite recruitment mechanism probably are examples of incremental change that have accumulated to the point of representing a qualitative alteration in the character of society. Undoubtedly, some would disagree with my classifications, but that is not the critical point. The more important issue is whether we can identify systematic differences between the two types of innovation and perhaps illuminate contrasting directions in which changes brought about through these two distinctly

Figure 1

Three Conceptions of Innovation

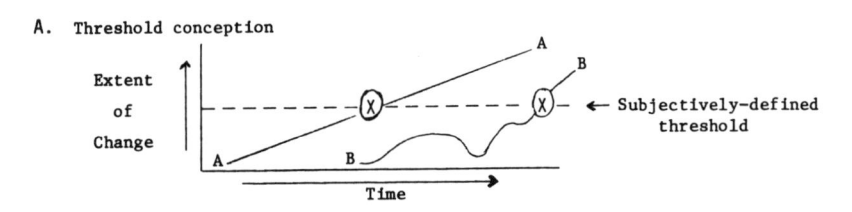

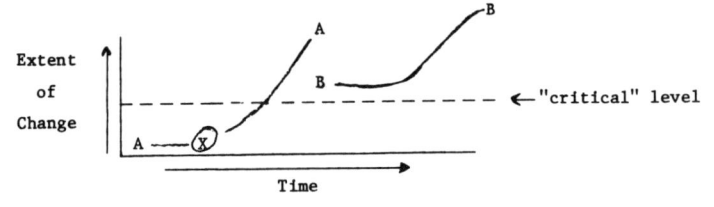

A. Threshold conception

Extent of Change ↑ ... ← Subjectively-defined threshold

Time →

B. Step-function conception (level-dependent)

Extent of Change ↑ ... ← "critical" level

Time →

C. Step-function conception (level-independent)

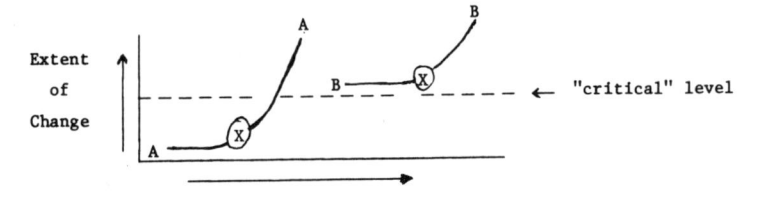

Extent of Change ↑ ... ← "critical" level

Ⓧ denotes occurrence of innovation

different processes might move in the future.

Some other issues are raised in the literature on innovation that warrant mention here. For example, do we wish to build contextual differences into our definitions of innovation? Specifically, will we accept the often-heard statement of the form, "That might not be an innovation in Poland, but it certainly is in Bulgaria"? If we believe that such contextual factors determine whether changes are really "innovative," then how are we to identify and measure the appropriate contextual factors that need to be examined?

Another important issue raised in the literature is the distinction between innovations that endure and innovations that fail within relatively short periods of time. For example, a little less than twenty years ago in the Soviet Union and some of the Eastern European countries, there was a distinct shift away from economic planning based entirely on sectoral considerations and toward planning with an important regional component. Furthermore, regional economic institutions were built up and made significantly more important in the administration of economic policy. I believe that most of us, viewing the situation at that time, felt that this was an innovative change. But it did not really endure; by 1965 the thinking had changed back to a distinct sectoral emphasis. What distinguishes innovations that fail from those that endure? What factors contribute to the success or failure of an innovation? To what extent are these factors characteristic of the innovation itself, and to what extent are they characteristic of the environment, including the individuals who must put the innovation into effect?

Yet another important question concerns the substantive essence of innovations. What should we be studying? The *objects* of innovation, that is, the structures themselves? The *uses* to which these new structures are to be put? The *purposes* for which they were initiated? For example, what is really significant about the role assigned in economic reform in the Soviet Union to the *khoziaistvenni raschot?* Surely it is not the object itself, since profit and loss statements have been submitted in Soviet industries since the late 1920s. Is the significant thing the role assigned to profit and loss statements, namely, their elevation to a position of much greater importance as a criterion for evaluating the performance of enterprises? Or should we be directing our attention to the reasons why the profit and loss statements have been accorded greater significance, a question that has a substantially more complex response? Perhaps the answer is that we should look at each dimension of innovations; but, at a minimum, we should be explicit about how we address the subject.

Another of our conference themes concerns the *diffusion* of innovation. Just as a great deal has been written about innovation, a good deal of work has been done on diffusion. For our purposes, some of the work on diffusion done by the anthropologist Raoul Naroll and his colleagues is particularly important.[3] Naroll distinguishes among what he calls hyper-diffusional, semi-diffusional, and functional cases. (Actually, Naroll calls functional cases "undiffusional.") Hyper-diffusional cases are circumstances in which the innovation moves from one place to another for reasons that are totally external to the recipient unit; presumably, there was no functional pressure within the recipient unit to innovate in this direction at all. Such an innovation may have been externally imposed, perhaps by force. The semi-diffusional case is the most realistic, but it is also the most difficult to break down into its two components. That is, semi-diffusional cases are *interactive* functional-diffusional cases, in which there is a combination of diffusion from without, and pressure for the adoption of the innovation within. Functional, or undiffusional, cases are those in which there is no identifiable pressure from without (and there may even be resistance from without) for the implementation of the innovation within a particular unit;

nevertheless, the innovation is undertaken.

It is important to consider how we can best assess the relative significance of external and internal pressures for the adoption of new policy practices. How can we go about separating out these three classes of cases, distinguishing among them in such a way that we can understand the implications of innovation in each of these three forms? Indeed, many of what still seem riddles to us in seeking an understanding of domestic economic and political change in Eastern Europe would be substantially resolved if we could systematically answer that question.

Another, more general, way to bring the literature on innovation and diffusion to bear on our considerations is simply to list the most important research focuses that have emerged in those literatures. Among the central questions raised in research on innovation and diffusion are the following:

1. What is the substance of the innovation?
2. Why was the innovation initiated?
3. How was the innovation initiated?
4. How and where was the innovation first adopted and implemented?
5. How has the innovation been evaluated?
6. How has the innovation spread?
7. Who are the adapters and the rejecters? What distinguishes them?
8. How have adapter attributes modified the innovation in place?
9. What is the ultimate resulting form and character of an innovation in a given location? What are its implications for (a) system structure; (b) system functioning; (c) the pattern of political values, beliefs, and attitudes; and (d) political behavior?

In my view, we should try to address each of these

questions with respect to each of the policy innovations we want to study. Aside from giving us guidance concerning the important dimensions of innovation, this checklist might help us connect our work back to other relevant research in a more explicit way.

Finally, it is worth pausing to emphasize a point that is by now clear to all of us who study socialist systems, namely, that there are enormous differences among the systems of Eastern Europe and the Soviet Union with respect to the nature of policy innovations that have taken place and with respect to the systemic or regime predisposition or inclination toward political or economic innovation. It seems important to retain attention to these differences and not to yield any more often that we must to the admittedly tempting tendency to speak of Eastern Europe, or socialist systems, as if they were an essentially homogeneous collectivity.

The Policy Sciences and Innovation in Socialist Systems

The focus of this chapter is on the policy sciences and the contribution that they can and do make to policy innovation in socialist systems. A word of clarification seems necessary at the outset. Two usages of the term *policy sciences* are evident in the literature. One is to define the policy sciences as the systematic study of policymaking. With due regard to the work that has been done in Yugoslavia for a number of years now, and to a lesser extent in recent years in Poland and Hungary, on the nature of economic decision making (and in Yugoslavia, on political decision making as well), I think it fair to say that the policy sciences in this sense are not especially well developed in socialist systems. The second usage is to refer to the policy-relevant outputs of scientific research. This substantially broader rendering of the notion of the policy sciences is what I have in mind here.

Factors Enhancing the Contribution of Science to Policy Innovation

There are six principal factors that, it seems to me, enhance the contribution of science to policy innovation in socialist systems. I have commented elsewhere on some of these and shall give only summary treatment to them here.[4] The first is the important role assigned to science in Marxist-Leninist doctrine. Loren Graham, in his important work on science in the Soviet Union, has argued that the philosophical orientation of Marxism-Leninism, embracing science as fully as it does, has manifested itself in a governmental commitment to science that is, in Graham's words, "unmatched in intensity by any other nation in the world."[5] And not only does Marxism-Leninism cast itself in scientific terms, it implicitly urges scientific thinking as a basis for understanding reality. Indeed, we know that science has been added to the official list of "means of production" in Marxist philosophy. Furthermore, science itself has become a kind of ideology of its own right, especially in the last twelve to fifteen years in the Soviet Union and in some Eastern European countries. A number of hefty tracts have been written discussing science as a world view. Similarly, a commitment to technology is a commitment to science; as a practical matter, I think there is general agreement that this commitment to technology has advanced at an extraordinary pace in the last three or four decades, especially in the Soviet Union.

Second, the historical role of scientific institutions in the societies now governed by communist parties tends to reinforce the importance of science. There has been a traditionally close relationship between the state and scientific enterprises, especially in the Soviet Union and Bulgaria. For example, from the founding of the Bulgarian Academy of Sciences, which took place in 1911, much of the leadership of the academy was active in government and politics; in fact, two presidents of the academy (Ivan Geshov and Bogdan Filov) were simultaneously head of state and head of the academy. There was a pattern of central funding and administration of science well before the establishment of communist governments in these countries. Scientific institutions have therefore always been assumed to have high ethical and practical responsibilities and obligations to the state to produce useful knowledge. The general picture is very much one of institutions that are to be listened to, because they are supposed to be producing, and because the tab is being picked up by the people who are doing the listening.

A third factor enhancing the contribution of science to policy innovation consists of the following developments: (1) the increasing complexity of the social and economic order, (2) the increasing need for technical expertise (including managerial competence), and (3) the salvation seen in technology as a means to overcome lagging starts and admittedly ineffective administrative practices in the process of economic and social growth. Many of us would probably suspect that this is the single most important factor that makes science so preeminent in these societies; it is an argument that has been frequently repeated, and I shall not elaborate it here.

Fourth, we should not forget that scientists are specialist elites. In these systems they operate in an elitist context, in which it is implicitly assumed that certain people have the right to speak out on certain kinds of questions—questions on which others should remain silent. The point seems so obvious that we may not appreciate its significance. We should keep in mind that things are not this way in every society; our own is perhaps the best example of the contrary condition. Specialist elites operating in essentially nonelitist systems are not accorded the automatic status that comes in systems that are essentially elitist in character.

Fifth, in my own view there is an inexorable movement in

socialist systems toward pragmatism and a problem-solving posture toward contentious issues of an economic and social nature. Orthodoxy—though not necessarily ideology—has declined dramatically in importance. Similarly, it seems to me that ideology is increasingly playing a rationalizing, as opposed to a prescriptive, function in decision making. The minor reversals of some of Khrushchev's flexible postures in both domestic and foreign policy do not alter, I believe, the basic fact that decision making is an increasingly bureaucratized, routinized, and pragmatically oriented process in the Soviet Union and elsewhere in Eastern Europe.

The final enhancing factor has to do with the increasing costs of acquiring information in highly complex, increasingly modern societies, in which an enormous bureaucracy attempts to administer a substantial proportion of human activity. Some theoretical literatures are again relevant here[6]—for example, on the characteristics of decision making taking place under a combination of three conditions: first, increased institutional and structural *complexity* resulting in the *insulation* (and sometimes isolation) of top decision makers; second, an increasing *uncertainty* in projections on the part of decision makers as to the likely outcomes of given courses of action; and third, an *acute lack of information,* resulting from the fact that social management generates a need for information that cannot be met without enormous financial and human costs.

I do not wish to oversimplify the thrust of the sometimes elegant decision theory literature. But there is one straightforward implication of much of this writing, namely, that decision making under the conditions just described tends to gravitate sharply toward the selective seeking of marginally efficient information. By "marginally efficient information" I do not mean information that is not really efficient, but in fact just the opposite. The concept refers to information that is efficient *at the margin;* that is, to information that has a high probability of yielding better understanding with the smallest possible investment. Now let me try to reconnect this line of argument to the general point being made—about the respects in which scientists have a kind of built-in policy-input advantage in highly bureaucratized systems. Marginally efficient information is most likely to come from specialist elites—from individuals who are known a priori to have expertise or special skills directly relevant to whatever the problem at hand might be. Access to these elites is rapid and low-cost, and in theory at least, the information obtained should be high in both quality and relevance. Thus the argument is that the very character of decision making in highly structured, highly bureaucratized systems leads to an increase in reliance on specialized sources of information.

Factors Limiting the Contribution of Science to Policy Innovation

At the same time, a number of factors limit the likely impact of scientific research on policy, especially influence that might bring about genuinely innovative change. First, scientists in state service, especially in service to a state that has operated over a relatively long period of time with a rather narrowly defined spectrum of acceptable ideological positions, are rather different from scientists whose connections with government are less direct. There is abundant evidence that Soviet and other East European scientists sometimes have conveyed information shaped largely by what they thought their political superiors wanted to hear. The scientific enterprise, like any societal institution, has instincts for self-survival; self-survival may call for steering the boat away from particularly stormy waters. Thus one has a strong suspicion that the neglect of social science by the Soviet regime until the last decade or so persisted in part because those people who, by professional training or inclination, might have been inclined to do "concrete social research" were just as happy not to be asked to do it.

Furthermore, even leaving aside the presumed policy-relevant values of the scientific community (which we commonly assume are different from those of practicing politicians—I shall return to this point in a moment), it may well be that the informational inputs received by policymakers from scientific research institutions serve, on balance, to reinforce the perspectives already held by policymakers. This is true in part because, espeically in the Soviet Union and Bulgaria, not only the nature of research tasks, but to a certain extent the methods to be employed in pursuing those tasks, are worked out collaboratively between research institutions and their governmental clients. Thus there is a very special sense in which the character of these societies, and the character of the relationship between the policy community and the scientific community, contribute to a check on the innovative thrust of scientific research. At the same time, one of the most important indicators of change in these societies in recent years is the fact that policymakers seem increasingly willing to ask questions, the answers to which are not in some sense preordained.

Second, the embedding of science within ideological doctrine in socialist systems may actually make more complicated, and in some respects less productive, the process of communication between researchers and policymakers. When all is said and done, I think it is clear that the scientist and the policymaker in any society talk in different kinds of terms, and to one degree or another they are motivated to undertake and to use the results of research in somewhat different ways. The central mission of science is presumably to identify dimensions of reality and to explain the processes by which these dimensions are altered over time. The task of the policymaker is to make consistent evaluations of certain past and contemporary practices and to attempt to mold the future environment in a particular direction. The committed scientist and the committed policymaker frequently may find that their respective points of view imply different behaviors. This seems especially likely in any system in which a pervasive official ideology structures the choice taking of policymakers.

Third, another irony present in the socialist systems of Western Europe and the Soviet Union is the fact that their initially "revolutionary" character actually engenders a certain resistance to change. Simply put, no one knows the danger of uncharted change better than do revolutionaries. I do not seriously wish to suggest that the societies of Eastern Europe can now be classified as "revolutionary." But the origins of these systems are, in at least a broad sense, revolutionary. At the same time, some of the most telling criticisms of these societies—initially by Trotsky, Djilas, and even, in a sense, in recent years by Adam Schaff[7]—have dealt with the numbing effect of inefficient political management on the visionary dreams with which the regimes were established. In the course of making the revolution, cumbersome bureaucracies for the protection of that revolution and for the carrying out of a comprehensive blueprint of social change were established. The very size and ineffective operation of these bureaucracies have begotten a resistance to innovative change that is, in itself, one of the principal reasons for ideological disillusionment on the part of some of the formerly faithful.

A fourth factor limiting the contribution of science to policy innovation is the relationship between situations in which there is ambiguous authority structure, on the one hand, and the likelihood of innovative change, on the other hand. At the outset, I urged that we should try to distinguish among the *sources* of innovation, especially in terms of external stimuli, joint external-internal origins, and wholly internal stimuli. In the present context, the problem takes the shape of questions about policy autonomy. One of the most obvious, but nonetheless interesting, developments in Eastern Europe has been the emergence of *different degrees* of internal and external policy autonomy on the part of the respective regimes. It is both a cause and a result of this differential development, and of the varying relations between the Soviet Union and each of the Eastern European countries, that policymakers within the junior partner states perceive themselves to be in a position of ambiguous authority. What they may *want* to do may be more or less clear; what *initiatives* they should take toward *innovation* are substantially less clear. Again, both common sense and a considerable amount of literature on decision making suggest that people in ambiguous authority circumstances tend to implement change only incrementally and cautiously. The probability of innovation in such circumstances is relatively low.

Fifth, it seems clear that different regimes in Eastern Europe have different orientations toward science. At least four distinct postures toward science can be identified: pure science, prestige, production, and problem solving.[8] The likelihood that science will contribute to genuinely innovative changes in policy varies a good deal, depending on how the regime sees the role of science. For example, under a *pure science* orientation, the ongoing impact of social science research is likely to be minimal, but we might expect periodic innovative impacts in natural and technical science areas. The *prestige* orientation stresses the importance of conduct and interaction with scientists from the West as well as the development of a few fields in which Soviet and East European scientists can excel. It is likely to lead to uneven scientific activity and probably somewhat unpredictable results, but it may well have innovative impacts coming either as spin-offs of international scientific accomplishments or, understandably, in areas where national resource commitment has been disproportionate. Under the *production* orientation, the impacts of scientific research are likely to be more immediate and consistent, but are probably less likely to be of a broad, genuinely innovative character. (I know that some of my Bulgarian colleagues disagree with this assessment.[9]) Finally, there is the *problem-solving* orientation, one in which the activities of scientific research institutions are structured only in a rather general way and in which the specific subjects of research and the methodologies to be employed are left largely to the discretion of the researchers. I would suppose that this orientation would have more consistent medium-range and long-range innovative payoffs, in the social sciences as well as in the natural and technical sciences. To contrast three scientific establishments, it seems to me that Hungary is employing a problem-solving mode, Bulgaria a production-oriented mode, and the Soviet Union a combination of prestige and production modes.

It hardly needs to be mentioned that there are certain "primitive terms"—some unchallengeable premises—that guide policymaking in socialist systems. I believe that the scope of these "primitives" is narrowing all the time, but the process is slow, and the remaining pool of primitives is still large. Many of these have to do with the role of central planning and with the size of the public sector.[10] These are obviously constraints, insofar as they preclude major innovation that would challenge the status of these sacred principles.

Finally, "value co-optation" serves as a factor limiting the likely innovative contribution of science. A good deal has been written in recent years about co-optation as an elite selection mechanism.[11] Some of this research has concluded that the most consistent and important predictors of elite values are recent career positions held—in contrast, for example, with social provenance. One of the interesting implications of this is that as personnel co-optation increases, "value co-optation" may take place. That is, as scientists and other specialists co-opted directly into policymaking positions may come to think more like policy functionaries and less like scientists. (The contrast should not be oversimplified, but the basic distinction seems defensible.) Thus, paradoxically, a mechanism that presumably has been a force for change in the Soviet Union and in some Eastern European countries—the increasing co-optation of specialists into political elite positions—may ultimately be accompanied by a value co-optation that may reduce the innovative impact of the presence of these individuals in policy-relevant positions.

Sources of Variance in the Science-Policy Nexus: Modes of Input

Two other sets of factors affect the likelihood that science will affect the formation of public policy in socialist systems. One concerns the *modes of input* through which the findings and recommendations of scientific researchers are communicated to policymakers. The other consists of the *elements of policy* (or the policy process) toward which scientific inputs are directed. Even among socialist systems, there seem to be substantial differences in both respects.

There are four principal modes of potentially innovative scientific input to policymaking. The first is through *advisory roles,* both formal and informal. *Formal* advisory roles refer to institutions or individuals who occupy formal positions from which informational inputs, the formulation of alternatives, and perhaps also recommendations, are anticipated. The individuals and institutions that occupy these formal advisory roles are relatively easy to identify. Similarly, it is not particularly difficult to identify the kinds of research they are doing. Identifying the nature of the informational inputs that they provide to government, or the kinds of policy recommendations they might make, is substantially more problematic.

Informal advisory roles are by their nature more difficult to identify. One of the most critical questions confronting students of the science-policy nexus in socialist systems concerns the extent to which such informal advisory roles have an ongoing functional character. That is, to what extent are they effectively institutionalized? My impression is that there are relatively few such informal roles in most Eastern European countries; most of the scientific research inputs to the policy process seem to take place through formal, explicit, and well-established informational channels.

Advisory roles as a mode of input are distinguished by the fact that they represent the generation of information as an *ongoing process:* research is presumably being carried out and information generated regardless of whether there are specific requests or other stimuli from government.

A second mode of input might be characterized as the *passive informational role.* Such roles may fall to the same types of individuals—scientific institutions and individual researchers—that perform advisory roles. What distinguishes the passive information mode, however, is that information is generated only when it is explicitly requested in specific situations. Thus scientific inputs are generated in an ad hoc way and on a variety of subjects that, for any given research institution or individual, may exhibit relatively little continuity over time. These passive informational roles may often be the most consequential, since they will often be occasioned by requests from policy agencies for information and recommendations in situations that are perceived to be of crisis or similarly serious proportions. Unfortunately for students of the science-policy nexus, the transmission of information and recommendations through such passive roles is far more difficult to trace.

Personnel *co-optation* is a third mode of input into the policy process. In this case, persons with specialized training, skills, and experience—usually in technical, managerial, or planning areas—are brought into formal policymaking positions. It is by now well demonstrated that the technique of co-optation is being used increasingly in socialist systems, especially the Soviet Union and the German Democratic Republic. Co-opted specialists are individuals who have established relatively slight involvement in, and commitment to, the party. We would logically expect—and research by Lodge[12] and Fleron[13] provides at least inferential evidence to this effect—that the basic values held by co-opted elites toward both the substance and process of policy might differ noticeably from those of recruited political functionaries who have occupied policy-relevant positions for a longer period of time. At the same time, we should not necessarily assume that the increasing presence of co-opted elites in the policy apparatus will lead to innovation in the substance or process of policy. In particular, we should keep in mind that recent research has demonstrated that current and recent positions held are frequently the best predictors of elite values and attitudes.[14] Thus, as was argued above, we might expect that co-opted specialist elites could with time acquire points of view increasingly similar to those of career policy functionaries. Still, it is reasonable to view co-opted elites among the most important potential carriers of innovation into the policy process. This is due in part to the fact that they bring whatever "innovative" ideas they may have directly into policymaking; that is, they do not have to communicate these ideas through the filters represented by more traditional recruited elites.

Career adaptation is a final mode of input that may bring innovation into policy. Western students of policymaking in socialist systems have given inadequate attention to career adaptation as a potential mechanism of political change. Most of the work done on leadership change in these societies has discussed only the distinctions between recruitment and co-optation as mechanisms of elite selection and promotion. Yet one of the system types identified in Fleron's important work on system change in the Soviet Union is the adaptive-monocratic system type.[15] One of the distinguishing features of the adaptive-monocratic type is that changes in elite skills necessitated by increasing modernity and complexity of the social order are effected not primarily by bringing in new individuals with needed skills, but by retraining existing elites, in effect bringing about reorientations of their careers.

The importance of looking carefully at career reorientation is suggested by a recent study of the Bulgarian elite.[16] There are two functional specializations which are being increasingly emphasized in the retraining of existing leaders: foreign policy, and the control specialization, or internal security function. My argument is that functional areas characterized by extensive career reorientation are areas in which there is likely to be the smallest amount of innovation resulting from scientific input. The reasoning is simply that these posts are being manned by longtime political functionaries, and relatedly, that the regime saw fit to place such individuals into these positions, rather than attempting to co-opt new blood from the outside.

Sources of Variance in the Science-Policy Nexus: Focuses of Inputs

It is likely that inputs from the scientific community will be more or less relevant to different aspects of the complex process of policymaking. Broadly, there are three types of impact that scientific inputs might have on policy: (1) impacts on the *substance* of policy; (2) impacts on the *processes* by which policy is made; and (3) impacts on the *policy infrastructure*—i.e., on the structures and rules that establish the parameters within which policy is formulated and that affect the ways in which the elements of the process are integrated and the ways in which substance and process are integrated.[17] We can imagine scientific activity affecting each of these aspects of policy and doing so in differing degrees at different times—and varying in impact among policy areas as well.

The first type of impact has primarily to do with the nature of the value-allocating outputs of government, the second has to do with the procedural dimensions of the distribution of power and influence in the policy; and the third is both coordinative-managerial and norm-defining in nature. Those specialists who have an impact on the first dimension of policy have been characterized as "ideological" advisors. Those who influence the second and third dimensions of policy have been called "technical" advisors. This sort of dichotomous rendering of advisory roles doubtless oversimplifies, but it does capture an essential distinction between influence on where the system is going, on the one hand, and on how it will get there, on the other.

Western students of socialist policymaking have been interested primarily in the first aspect of policy influence— i.e., the impact of science on the substance of policy. This influence probably is easier to identify and in any case is likely to manifest itself more clearly in a shorter period of time. That is, the "lag" between influence stimulus and policy change can be expected to be shorter where the stimulus directly affects policy substance, rather than process.

On the other hand, the longer-run significance of impacts on process and infrastructure may be substantially greater. Process and infrastructure are harder to modify, especially in highly structured systems where basic models of political organization are expressly prescribed by an official doctrine. Thus the impacts of scholarly communication may well require a longer time to become visible in these areas. But any such effects on process and infrastructure may be presumed to affect whatever substantive policy choices are made within them in the future. Furthermore, just as processual and infrastructural influences are harder to bring about, they will be more difficult to discard. Thus there is good reason to think that we should be interested at least as much in process and in infrastructure as in policy substance. Unfortunately, influences on process and infrastructure are more difficult to chart.

An Assessment: Two Innovative Contributions of the Policy Sciences

It seems to me that in the socialist systems with which I am familiar, there are two policy areas in which the scientific contribution to policy innovation may be most substantial. One of these is in influencing the ways in which government provides basic public goods and services to citizens. The second is rather more problematic and substantially more difficult to examine systematically: it consists of helping decision makers understand the contexts in which they are making political choices and the implications of those choices for the basic character of the system on whose behalf they are acting.

With respect to the first category—scientific impact on the provision of basic public goods and services—I think the evidence is ample that research institutions in Bulgaria, Poland, Hungary, and the Soviet Union have a great deal of importance. They are involved in the definition of population needs; in developing mechanisms for monitoring these needs and for understanding the nature of population demands; in the formulation of norms, standards, and guidelines for health, sanitation, and housing (and I might add that in Hungary, for example, the three research institutes working on these kinds of questions have come up with distinctly different recommendations concerning norms and standards); in the design of the structures by which such services as health care are delivered; and in the measurement of ways in which the population uses the services that are provided and is affected precisely by their use of these services. I cannot stress too strongly that although these kinds of activities may not be as glamorous or as headline-grabbing as, for example, activities in the foreign policy area, there is good reason to believe that the effect of such programs on the everyday lives of the human beings living in these societies is probably greater than is the impact of the scientific input on the conduct of foreign policy.

Perhaps I am unduly under the sway of the kind of work that I was involved in at IIASA,[18] but I have a strong feeling that it is in the area of the delivery of public goods and services, more than in any other single area, that scientific research institutions in socialist systems can have a distinct impact on policy and can contribute to a substantial improvement in the character of human existence in those societies.

It is far more difficult to understand the impact of scientific research institutions on decision makers' perceptions of what they themselves are doing. The four points I want to develop briefly in this connection essentially describe what I believe scientists are *trying to do* in Hungary, in particular, in the Soviet Union as well, and perhaps to a somewhat lesser extent in Bulgaria and Poland. It is frankly very difficult to tell yet whether they are succeeding.

First, scientists to whom policymakers apparently listen in countries such as Hungary are emphasizing the importance of including in decisional inputs information from sources of varying ideological posture. This applies both to internal and foreign sources of information. These scientists are trying to demonstrate the intrinsic value of communicating across ideological sets. The importance of this class of communication has not always been obvious to policymakers in Eastern Europe, as we are all very much aware. My own view—and it is very impressionistic—is that those scientists who look beyond a strict task-orientation in Eastern Europe (and I believe that many of them do) are trying very hard to make this fundamental point about ideologically broadened communication to policymakers.

Second, it is clear that in Hungary, and in Poland as well (to say nothing of Yugoslavia, where there is something of a tradition of such research), scholars are now studying the results of systematizing and routinizing political choice taking. Such routinization is, of course, a classic component of increasingly complex and large bureaucracy. What has especially distinguished routinization in socialist systems has been the failure to appreciate many of its consequences. Now there are scholars who are attempting to elaborate these implications. My impression is that such efforts from the scientific community have had some importance in the formal and informal efforts in Hungary to achieve some decentralization of economic planning and administration.

Third, there now seems little doubt that, perhaps especially in the more developed socialist systems of Eastern Europe, scientists are assuming important roles as "technological gatekeepers." We have already indirectly alluded to this function in talking about the importance of technical expertise in an increasingly complex and technologically oriented society. What I want to stress here is that both social and natural scientists are aware of this potential gatekeeper function and that they are now beginning to consider the ethical implications of locking and unlocking the gate, or of how far it should be left ajar at any particular hour.

Finally, one of the most consistent inadequacies in social and economic planning in socialist countries has been the failure to assess system capabilities accurately. I certainly do not want to imply that targets outlined in five-year plans have always been thought to be realistic; on the contrary, I believe that Western students of socialist economic decision making have consistently overstated the seriousness with which these plans are taken in those systems. At the same time, a substantial amount of misinformation has been involved in the formulation of these plans, and only in the last few years have Soviet and other East European economic planners begun to appreciate the magnitude of the informational problem they have and the severity of some of their errors of projected system capacity. There is ample evidence that scientific research institutes in Bulgaria, Hungary, and the Soviet Union are being turned to increasingly for detailed elaborations of the capabilities of these systems—not only for economic and social growth, but also for the development of certain specific categories of material and intellectual capacity, for example, education and manpower training programs. For example, the Bulgarians are deeply interested in this last question and are investing substantial personnel time in such studies.

The thrust of what this chapter has tried to convey can be summarized briefly. Perhaps I can restate the points I tried to make in reverse order. First, there are at least two critical areas in which the influence of scientific research institutions on policymaking is already identifiable in the socialist systems of Eastern Europe and the Soviet Union and is likely to increase in the future. I am less sanguine about our ability to trace the impact of scientific activity on policymaking in other areas, especially about our ability to identify its impact on foreign policy decisions. Second, the relationships between the policy sciences and policy innovation are very complex; there are a number of powerful factors operating in both directions, both limiting and enhancing the contribution of science to policy innovation. My urging is that we try to think as systematically as we can about what the sources of strength and weakness in scientific inputs to policy really are. Third, finally, I argued initially that we should be a good deal more careful than we usually are in defining terms such as *innovation, diffusion,* and *change.* Definitions are not semantic trivia; they are the cornerstones of communication. Related to this is my concern that when we talk about such things as policy innovation, and the diffusion of new ideas across space, we take into consideration the abundant existing theoretical literatures that treat these general phenomena. There has been a strong tendency in the field of communist studies to proceed atheoretically, with the notion that the special character of the places we were studying and the special magnitude of the data problems we confront somehow justify our being less rigorous, less systematic about what we do. I do not accept this, and in fact I think we have an obligation to look under at least the most promising intellectual rocks for clues that might help us better understand the very important nexus between science and the development of public policy.

Notes

1. Although now somewhat dated, the best single survey of innovation and diffusion studies, particularly as applied to the social sciences, is Everett M. Rogers and F. Floyd Shoemaker, *Communication of Innovations* (New York: Free Press, 1971).

2. William A. Welsh and G. Stephen Hirst, "Diffusion, Innovation, and Spatial Autocorrelation: Some Methodological Issues for Political Science" (Paper read at annual meetings of the American Political Science Association, Chicago, 1974).

3. For example, see Raoul Naroll, "Two Solutions to Galton's Problem," *Philosophy of Science* 28 (1961): 16-39; Raoul Naroll and Roy G. D'Andrade, "Two Further Solutions to Galton's Problem," *American Anthropologist* 65 (1963): 1053-1067; Raoul Naroll, "A Fifth Solution to Galton's Problem," *American Anthropologist* 66 (1964): 863-867; idem, "Galton's Problem: The Logic of Cross-Cultural Analysis," *Social Research* 32 (Winter 1965): 428-451.

4. William A. Welsh, "The Policy Sciences in Socialist Systems" (Paper read at annual meetings of the American Association for the Advancement of Slavic Studies, St. Louis, 1976).

5. Loren R. Graham, "The Development of Science Policy in the Soviet Union," in *Science Policies of Industrial Nations*, ed. T. Dixon Long and Christopher Wright (New York: Praeger, 1973), p. 12.

6. Unfortunately, the insights provided by the organization theory and decision theory literatures have rarely been focused on an understanding of organizational behavior in highly structured socialist systems. There are a few exceptions in some of the chapters in Carmelo Mesa-Lago and Carl Beck, eds., *Comparative Socialist Systems* (Pittsburgh: University Center for International Studies, 1976). One especially important aspect of organizational structure in Eastern Europe—the asymmetry of allocations of *authority* and *responsibility* at given levels of an organization—is treated, though in the abstract, in Kenneth J. Arrow, *The Limits of Organization* (New York: Norton, 1974).

7. Adam Schaff, *Marxism and the Human Individual* (New York: McGraw-Hill, 1970).

8. Welsh, "The Policy Sciences," pp. 25-29, treats these four orientations in more detail.

9. My conversations with Bulgarian researchers at a number of research institutes in Sofia during the spring of 1976 persuaded me that there is substantial commitment to what I have called the "production orientation" within the scholarly community and that probable payoffs—both short-run and longer-run—are thought to be advantages of this posture.

10. For a discussion of some of the common—and often misleading—Western assumptions about the nature of central planning under socialism, see Benjamin N. Ward, *The Socialist Economy: A Study of Organizational Alternatives* (New York: Random House, 1967); and William A. Welsh, "The Comparative Study of Public Policy: Some Methodological Issues" (manuscript, 1976).

11. For example, see Carl Beck, Frederick J. Fleron, Jr., Milton Lodge, Derek J. Waller, William A. Welsh, and M. George Zaninovich, *Comparative Communist Political Leadership* (New York: David McKay, 1973), especially the chapters by Fleron and Lodge.

12. Ibid.; see also Milton Lodge, *Soviet Elite Attitudes since Stalin* (Columbus, Ohio: Charles E. Merrill, 1969).

13. Frederick J. Fleron, Jr., "System Attributes and Career Attributes: The Soviet Political Leadership System, 1952 to 1965," in Beck et al., *Comparative Communist Political Leadership*, pp. 43-85.

14. Lewis J. Edinger and Donald D. Searing, "Social Background in Elite Analysis: A Methodological Inquiry," *American Political Science Review* 61, no. 2 (1967): 428-445; Donald D. Searing, "The Comparative Study of Elite Socialization," *Comparative Political Studies* 1, no. 4 (1969): 471-500. For a review of some recent research relevant to this theme and dealing directly with socialist systems, see William A. Welsh, "Elites and Leaders in Communist Systems: Some New Perspectives," *Studies in Comparative Communism* 9, nos. 1-2 (1976): 162-186.

15. Fleron, "System Attributes."

16. William A. Welsh, "Stability and Change in Bulgarian Political Leadership, 1944-1971" (Paper read at a conference on "Social Stratification and the Roles of Political Elites in East-Central Europe," University of Kansas, Lawrence, Kansas, 1972).

17. One of the most consistent oversimplifying assumptions made by Western students of policymaking under socialism is that the basic policy process is insensitive to variations in substance—

i.e., that the process is essentially the same regardless of the substance of the policy issues being handled. There is good reason to believe that this is not the case—it certainly does not hold for nonsocialist systems—and there is a consequent need to direct attention to the ways in which the substance of issues being processed affects the process itself.

18. At the International Institute for Applied Systems Analysis, in Laxenburg, Austria, researchers from the Soviet Union, Eastern Europe, North America, and Japan are working together on critical common problems. Many of these are in natural and technical science fields—energy, ecology, water conservation—but some are in the social and medical sciences. In this latter category, important research is being done on regional economic and social development, population growth and movement, and the delivery of health care.

2. Political Groupings and Their Role in the Process of Change in Eastern Europe

Roger E. Kanet

During the past decade, Western students of the European socialist systems have increasingly been concerned with the problems that some of these "modern" industrial societies have with the ability of ruling communist parties to adapt to the demands of a differentiated industrial society, and with the role of groups in socialist societies.[1] Authors such as Zvi Gitelman and Andrzej Korbonski have argued that the socioeconomic development that has occurred in Eastern Europe during the postwar period—in part, at least, as the result of the policy choices of the political elite—has led to socioeconomic changes that, in turn, have created new social and employment differentiation, new demands on the political elite, and new sources of social and political conflict.[2]

Although Western scholars generally agree that economic growth has brought new problems for the socialist ruling elites, they are far less unanimous about the ability of those elites to respond effectively to these new problems. Korbonski, for example, is rather optimistic that gradual change in the political systems of Eastern Europe will open up political systems to participation from groups outside the present elite.[3] Others, such as Zygmunt Bauman and Melvin

Croan, are much more sanguine about the prospects for an expanded political role for groups and individuals outside the leadership positions of the ruling communist parties.[4]

Western scholars have disagreed not only about the prospects for an opening up of the political process, but also about the development of political groups and their role in the policymaking process in socialist countries. H. Gordon Skilling, David Lane, Korbonski, and others have argued that during the post-Stalin period, interest groups have emerged and have been able to play a positive role in the political process.[5] On the other hand, others, such as Andrew Janos and Franklyn Griffiths, caution that such groups in socialist societies are not the same as organized interest groups in the West.[6]

In the present chapter I hope to show that in spite of the restrictions placed upon them by the political authorities, "political groupings" have emerged in socialist countries and that one can examine both the evolution of these "groupings" and the impact they have had in stimulating political and economic changes in socialist systems.

In this chapter, *change* will be used rather than the more specific term *innovation,* which refers to change that involves the purposive creation and implementation of an institutionalized policy or program.[7] *Change*—as used in this chapter—refers to two distinct, but interrelated, processes. On the one hand, it will characterize the economic growth, industrialization, and urbanization that have occurred in socialist states during the last thirty years. In this sense, *change* is virtually synonymous with modernization and signifies the economic, social, and intellectual transformation of society by industrialization.[8] This concept also implies an "end state" (though one that is constantly modified) namely, "modern" society, which is characterized by high levels of industrialization and urbanization.

However, the term *change* will also be used more narrowly

with regard to the political systems of the socialist states and the movement away from the highly centralized authoritarian systems created in the Stalinist era. Following Janos, we shall distinguish three separate processes of political change in Eastern Europe: (1) the rationalization, or bureaucratization, of revolutionary regimes; (2) the decentralization, or liberalization, of bureaucratic politics; and (3) the democratization, or pluralization, of authoritarian systems.[9]

The other major term in this analysis is *political groupings*. *Political groupings* (rather than the more familiar *interest groups*) underscores the differences between political groupings as they have evolved in the socialist states and political interest groups in Western liberal democracies. Those who have argued for the use of interest group theory in the study of communist political systems have been strongly criticized. However, something like interest groups has evolved in several East European countries, and their activities are important both for the functioning of the area's political systems and for our understanding of those systems. *Political groupings* refers to aggregates of persons who possess certain common characteristics, share certain attitudes on public issues, adopt distinct positions on these issues, and make definite demands on those in authority. It is not assumed that these groupings are organized into institutionalized pressure groups of the Western variety, although such openly organized groups have recently appeared in socialist states. Nor is it assumed that these groupings necessarily are as lasting as interest groups in the West are. Finally, it is not assumed that the existence and activity of political groupings are independent from at least the tacit permission of the political elite. Interest groupings can be and have been suppressed in socialist states, and, given a political environment that denies legitimacy to all nonofficial organizations, their very existence is a challenge to the system and depends largely on the regime's unwillingness to pay the political costs of eliminating them.

Critics of interest group theory (such as Janos and Griffiths) are correct in noting that "interest groups" in communist states lack many of the characteristics of interest groups in the West. However, these "interest groups"—groups of individuals separate from the official political elite and attempting to influence policy—do exist in Eastern Europe. They can exist within the official administrative apparatus with recognition by the regime—Jerry Hough refers to this as "institutional pluralism"[10]—or they can exist outside the official political system and either oppose the system itself or attempt to influence its policy choices.

Even though these groupings differ from political interest groups in the West, they are definitely political—in at least four different senses.[11] First, they may be political if they have a base of support within the existing political structures. In Eastern Europe such groupings, or "institutional interest groups," although a part of the official political elite, attempt through organized action of various sorts to influence the policy process. Second, they may be political because of their goals. In the socialist states these groupings' major purpose is to influence public policy choices or the structure of the political system itself. Third, they may be political because of their methods. These methods may, for example, focus on efforts to influence either policymaking or policy implementation and range from petitions to the political elite all the way to illegal activity, such as strikes and riots. Finally, they may be political if their actions, although primarily nonpolitical, have an effect on the political system itself.

The major argument of this chapter is that socioeconomic change, or modernization, has had a major impact on the socialist societies and that one of the results of this impact has been an increased differentiation of society. This, in turn, has resulted in the development of groups with shared attitudes and goals, which, though outside the formal political elite, have made demands on that elite. These "political groupings" have on occasion even played an active role in the political process itself. In developing the argument, I shall place special emphasis on political groupings in three of the socialist states—Czechoslovakia, Hungary, and Poland.

The Development of Political Groupings in the European Socialist States

Several authors have examined the impact of the socialist countries' drive for industrialization on the development of social and occupational groups.[12] These authors have noted how the social structure has changed along with economic growth, industrialization, and urbanization. Although the countries of Eastern Europe, with the exception of the GDR and the Czech lands, were predominantly agricultural before World War II, by 1970 all of them had made significant gains on all of the indexes usually employed to measure modernization, including education, industrialization, urbanization, and medical care. However, not only have certain social groups—such as an industrial working class and the technical intelligentsia—been created or enlarged as a result of this process, but a number of more traditional cleavages have continued to exist in some of the socialist states. In Czechoslovakia the differences between Czechs and Slovaks have not been eradicated, and in Poland the political role of the Roman Catholic Church has been reemphasized by such recent developments as the June 1976 price riots.

In every East European country socioeconomic development has substantially increased both the size and the role of the "socialist" intelligentsia—as opposed to the prewar educated middle classes. Increased educational opportunities, the expansion of the bureaucracy, the need for a managerial class to run the newly created state industries—these and other factors have played an important role in the creation of what contemporary Marxist-Leninist theory refers to as the "stratum of mental workers." In addition, industrialization has considerably enlarged the urban working class, which in large measure had not existed before World War II. On various occasions during the past two decades, sectors of these new social groups have become politicized and, in certain circumstances, have played an active role in the political process.

So far we have spoken only of social or occupational groups that have emerged in Eastern Europe as a result of economic development and urbanization. More important for the question of the relationship of social and occupational groups to the political process, however, are the means by which social groups evolve into political groupings with similar interests and attitudes and the conditions under which they are likely to attempt to influence the political process. During the Stalinist period, the tight control over society and the use of police and terror tactics prevented the emergence of any political grouping outside the narrow confines of the ruling party. However, over the course of the past twenty years, on virtually every occasion when the central political leadership has loosened its hold on society, unofficial political activity has developed both within and outside the party.

The clearest example occurred in Czechoslovakia during the reform period. By mid-1968 a variety of political groupings had emerged, most of which were not only creating formal organizations, but also attempting to influence political development in Czechoslovakia.[13] In Poland serious political and economic problems have on several occasions resulted in the emergence of groupings that have succeeded in influencing the political process—the most recent example being the creation and activity of the Workers' Defense Committee (KOR). Despite government harassment, this organization has attempted to change government policy regarding the workers arrested during the strikes of June 1976. In fact, its demands actually go beyond the events of June 1976, for it is in effect calling for a new relationship between the state apparatus and society at large—for a form of governmental accountability to the populace that has generally been lacking in socialist states.

One of the most interesting and important developments in the post-Stalin era has been the unwillingness or inability of the East European political elite to resort to repressive measures in dealing with dissent and unofficial attempts to influence the policymaking process, the measure that proved most effective during the Stalin era. Not only have groupings outside the party attempted to influence official policy, but also individuals within the party organization have been actively involved in some of these efforts. In fact, the greatest change and reform have come when a substantial number of party and state officials have joined in efforts aimed at political change—e.g., the research economists working in party and government research institutes played a major role in the reform movement in Czechoslovakia during the mid-1960s.[14]

Political Groupings and Political Change

As noted (following the distinction made by Janos), political change in Eastern Europe in the post-Stalin years consists of three separate processes: (1) the bureaucratization of revolutionary regimes, (2) the decentralization of bureaucratic polities, and (3) the pluralization of authoritarian systems. Here we are concerned primarily with the last two types of changes, namely, modification of the rigid centralization of authority and a devolution of political power to subnational units, as well as the expansion of participation in the political process to "unofficial" political groupings outside the present political elite.

The noted Polish sociologist Jan Szczepański has stated:

> Another unorganized but politically significant force is that of interest groups which, in pursuing their objectives,

try to influence political and economic decisions in order to make them more profitable for their members. There are no organized lobbies in socialist society, but interest groups use various ways and means of applying pressure to the decision-making bodies.... As an example, however, one can cite intellectuals who use various forms of pressure to obtain more freedom of expression and a higher proportion of the national income.... There are some professional groups, for example, the technical intelligentsia and economists, that vie for influence on the thinking of the Politburo in order to push through their own ways of socialist construction and to safeguard their professional interests. Managers of socialized enterprises also strive to get more autonomy and to broaden the scope of their decisions.

It must be stressed that these groups do not fight for political power and do not aim to replace the group in power, but rather try to influence its decisions.[15]

Much the same can probably be said of all of the European socialist countries, although the degree to which political groupings actually operate does differ from country to country. The clearest examples of how the various elements of the intelligentsia influence policy can be seen in the various reform movements of the 1960s. In Czechoslovakia the role of economists, writers, and labor unions in pushing forward the reform program while at the same time attempting to guarantee their own interests has been clearly documented. These groupings unquestionably perceived themselves as political groups with common interests and attitudes and used all means available to them in order to influence the political elite. To a substantial degree they were successful—until the Soviet intervention interrupted the processes of reform and change.

In the GDR, as Thomas Baylis has argued, economists and party and state technical officials "functioned, clearly, as a pressure group in favor of Libermanism."[16] The introduction of the GDR's New Economic System in the mid-1960s was largely the result of a technical elite's successful "lobbying" against the opposition of a large part of the state bureaucracy. In Hungary the parliamentary discussions before the introduction of the New Economic Mechanism in 1968 involved a similar pattern of lobbying.[17]

These political groupings that have tried to influence the policy process are groupings largely within the existing system that play the role of expert advisors to the political elite. Their goal has been primarily the decentralization of the bureaucratic economic and political systems. This was especially true of the economists in the reform movements in both Czechoslovakia and Hungary in the 1960s. Their methods were limited primarily to persuasion of the political elite, although in Czechoslovakia the rapid development of the reform movement during 1968 resulted in the emergence of groupings that were able to gain access to other resources—i.e., the media—in presenting their demands for the democratization of Czechoslovak society.

In Poland during the past two decades, several interest groupings have tried to move the system toward decentralization and democratization. The first such groupings appeared in 1956-1957 and played a major role in moving Poland away from the Stalinist model toward a more liberal society. This change was short-lived, and the years 1957 through 1968 can be viewed as a period of gradual "normalization" in Polish society.[18] Members of the intelligentsia, students, workers, and the church played a role in the events that led to Gomulka's return to power and the introduction of a program of liberalization. There is little question that these groupings had common interests and employed political means in order to accomplish political goals. Although their successes did not last and their role was gradually undermined, they, for a time at least, were able to have an impact on the structure of the political system itself.

In December 1970, during the riots in Gdańsk and other Baltic cities, Polish workers again made demands for both economic and political changes. In his discussion of worker demands, David Lane argues that "the riots in Gdańsk were fundamentally the activity of a stratum of the working class which was conscious of the fact that its place in society was determined by its relationship to the means of production and that its well-being could be enhanced by collective action. Its aims were explicitly political and economic."[19] Even though the major demands had to do with wages, the rising cost of living, and related economic matters, the workers also demanded changes that were clearly political. Most of these concerned greater participation in the political system, in particular as this related to workers' interests.[20]

The most recent worker unrest in Poland—the strikes and riots associated with the aborted price increase of June 1976—has acted as a stimulus to the emergence of political groupings that have a number of common goals. Although the sole purpose of the strikes and riots of June 25 was to rescind the announced price increases, the subsequent treatment of the strikers—arrests, alleged beatings by police officials, and mass firings—led eventually to the development of a Polish civil rights movement. Most important in this respect was the Workers' Defense Committee (KOR), which was created in September 1976 to assist the workers dismissed and arrested in June 1976. In May 1977, however, the KOR expanded its activities and established an Intervention Bureau to collect and publicize information on officials' violations of human rights and a Social Defense Fund to assist the victims of official reprisals. Finally, in late September 1977, the restructuring of the committee under a new name—The Committee for Social Self-Defense "KOR" —was announced. The communique issued at the time of the reorganization stated:

> We shall continue our action because we are convinced that the most successful weapon against the domination of rules is the active solidarity of citizens, for the major cause of lawlessness by the authorities lies in the helplessness of the public, deprived of institutions independent of the state that

can protect the rights of individuals and groups, in keeping with their interests.[21]

According to the communique, the tasks of the restructured organization will include:

1. combating reprisals imposed for political, philosophical, religious, or racial reasons, as well as providing aid to persons persecuted for these reasons;
2. combating lawless practices and providing aid to those suffering from them;
3. fighting for institutional guarantees of civic rights and freedoms;
4. supporting and defending all social initiatives aimed at implementing human and civic rights.[22]

In addition to the Workers' Defense Committee, other groups were active in Poland during 1976-1977. Most important was the Catholic church, which has openly and repeatedly supported both the rights of the workers fired and jailed in June 1976 and the general principles to which the KOR was dedicated. In fact church activities in this area began two months before the creation of the Workers' Defense Committee.[23] Groups of students have also supported the rights of the workers, although their activities have brought action against some of them.[24] Finally, a second civil rights organization—The Movement for the Defense of Human and Civil Rights—was created in March 1977. Its members, unlike most of the KOR activists, are not primarily Marxists, although the goals of the two organizations seem to be similar.[25]

It would be difficult to prove that the activities of these political groupings have influenced government policy. However, some of their demands have been met, such as the eventual release of all of the workers who had been jailed in June 1976. It would appear that the activities of the KOR, the church, and others helped influence the behavior of the political elite.

The groupings that have emerged once again in Poland certainly fit our definition of political groupings: they consist of aggregates of persons who share attitudes on certain public issues who have adopted distinct positions on these issues, and who have been addressing demands to those in authority. Their goals, methods, and the implications of their actions are political in nature. They are by no means interest groups in the Western sense, for they lack legitimacy, independent organizational resources, and access to local media—characteristics of effective interest groups. Yet in spite of the restrictions placed on them by the absence of such "political resources" and in spite of the harassment suffered at the hands of party and state officials, these groupings have continued to formulate and express their demands.

The primary question of this chapter concerns the role of political groupings in effecting change in socialist societies and their impact on either the decentralization of bureaucratic polities or the growth of pluralism in the political process itself. The reform movements of the 1960s, in which various groupings of the intelligentsia were prominent, did have as one of their purposes the decentralization of the economic decision-making process and the political mobilization of a broader spectrum of society. This phenomenon was especially obvious in Czechoslovakia, where both inside and outside the party the call for decentralization and democratization was effectively asserted. The present demands of such groupings as Charter 77 in Czechoslovakia and the Committee for Social Defense "KOR" in Poland, although aimed at specific issues, are calls for restructuring socialist politics. The ultimate goals of these groupings include the right to dissent, the accountability of state officials to society, the right to organize politically, and the creation of a pluralistic political system in which all groupings—not merely the official party elite—will have an opportunity to share in the policymaking process.

Political Groupings and the Future of Eastern Europe

As we have seen, political groupings have evolved within Eastern Europe over the past quarter century and have, on occasion, had an important influence on the political system. In general, however, the political elite in socialist states has maintained its dominant position: only when the political elite itself is divided have political groupings been able to exert effective influence on the policymaking process. Recent evidence indicates that the East European regimes are continuing to repress all efforts aimed at the creation of pluralistic political systems. The campaigns against political dissidents in Poland and Czechoslovakia demonstrate that the present leadership is not willing to extend participation to groups outside the elite unless absolutely forced to do so.

However, it is also important to note that because of several factors, the socialist governments have treated political groupings, including the dissidents, more leniently than in the Stalin era. The first, and probably most important, factor is a certain "mellowing" of the system over time—at least with regard to the use of the terrorist methods. In addition, détente, the Helsinki agreements, and an increased concern for world opinion (as well as for access to Western trade credits) have moderated the regimes' treatment of political opposition. In the long run, the political elites are probably fighting a losing battle. As modernization goes on, differentiation will continue and groups with demands opposing the wishes of the political elite will also continue to emerge. This process will assert itself only within society but also in the ruling party. Eventually the party elite will have to deal with these groups' demands for participation or else suffer the consequences of political instability.

Notes

1. The two most important recent contributions to the discussion of political development in Eastern Europe are Charles

Gati, ed., *The Politics of Modernization in Eastern Europe: Testing the Soviet Model* (New York-Washington-London: Praeger, 1974); and Jan F. Triska and Paul M. Cocks, eds., *Political Development in Eastern Europe* (New York-Washington-London: Praeger, 1977).

2. Zvi Gitelman, "Beyond Leninism: Political Developments in Eastern Europe," *Newsletter on Comparative Studies of Communism* 5, no. 3 (1972): 18-43; and idem, *The Diffusion of Political Innovation: From Eastern Europe to the Soviet Union*, Comparative Politics Series, vol. 3, no. 27 (Beverly Hills, Calif.: Sage Publications, 1972); Andrzej Korbonski, "Bureaucracy and Interest Groups in Communist Societies: The Case of Czechoslovakia," *Studies in Comparative Communism* 4 (1971): 57-79; idem, "Comparing Liberalization Processes in Eastern Europe: A Preliminary Analysis," *Comparative Politics* 4 (1972): 231-249; idem, "The Pattern and Method of Liberalization," in *Comparative Socialist Systems: Essays on Politics and Economics* ed. Carmelo Mesa-Lago and Carl Beck (Pittsburgh: University of Pittsburgh Center for International Studies, 1975). Since the recently published literature on political development, modernization, and change in communist systems has expanded almost exponentially, it will not be possible in this essay to refer to more than a very limited selection. For a useful introduction to this literature, see Lawrence L. Whetten, *Current Research in Comparative Communism: An Analysis and Bibliographic Guide to the Soviet System* (New York-Washington-London: Praeger, 1976).

3. Andrzej Korbonski, "The Prospects for Change in Eastern Europe," *Slavic Review* 33 (1974): 219-239. For similar views, see many of the articles included in Triska and Cocks, *Political Development in Eastern Europe*.

4. See Zygmunt Bauman, "Twenty Years After: The Crisis of Soviet-Type Systems," *Problems of Communism* 20, no. 6 (1971): 45-53; Melvin Croan's rejoinder to the Korbonski article cited in note 3, "Some Constraints on Change in Eastern Europe," *Slavic Review* 33 (1974): 240-245.

5. See H. Gordon Skilling, "Interest Groups and Communist Politics," *World Politics* 18 (1966): 435-461; idem, "Interest Groups and Communist Politics: An Introduction," in *Interest Groups in Soviet Politics*, ed. H. Gordon Skilling and Franklyn Griffiths (Princeton, N.J.: Princeton University Press, 1971). The most recent and most complete of Skilling's treatments of the

question of interest groups can be found in his monumental *Czechoslovakia's Interrupted Revolution* (Princeton, N.J.: Princeton University Press, 1976), pp. 493-613. See also David Lane, "The Role of Social Groups," in *Social Groups in Polish Society*, ed. David Lane and George Kolankiewicz (New York: Columbia University Press, 1973); and Korbonski, "Bureaucracy and Interest Groups in Communist Societies."

6. Andrew C. Janos, "Group Politics in Communist Society: A Second Look at the Pluralistic Model," in *Authoritarian Politics in Modern Society: The Dynamics of Established One-Party Systems*, ed. Samuel P. Huntington and Clement H. Moore (New York: Basic Books, 1970); Franklyn Griffiths, "A Tendency Analysis of Soviet Policy-Making," in Skilling and Griffiths, *Interest Groups in Soviet Politics*. See also Francis G. Castles, "Interest Articulation: A Totalitarian Paradox," *Survey* (London), no. 73 (1969), pp. 116-132.

7. This definition is slightly different from that used by Gitelman in *The Diffusion of Political Innovation*, p. 11. See also Lawrence A. Brown, "Innovation Diffusion in a Developing Economy: A Mesoscale View," *Economic Development and Social Change* 21 (1973): 274-292. In his "Policy Science as an Innovative Area in Socialist Systems," in this volume, William A. Welsh also refers to the distinction between *change* and *innovation*.

8. For a discussion of this process, see my "Modernizing Interaction within Eastern Europe," in Gati, *The Politics of Modernization in Eastern Europe*, pp. 278-282.

9. See Andrew C. Janos, "Systemic Models and the Theory of Change in the Comparative Study of Communist Politics," in *Authoritarian Politics in Communist Europe: Uniformity and Diversity in One-Party States*, ed. Andrew C. Janos (Berkeley, Calif.: Institute of International Studies, 1976): 25-26.

10. Jerry F. Hough, "The Soviet System: Petrification or Pluralism?" *Problems of Communism* 21, no. 2 (1972): 27-28.

11. I wish to express my debt to William A. Welsh for this distinction, made at the workshop at which the articles in this volume were originally presented.

12. See, for example, Jaroslav Krejčí, *Social Change and Stratification in Postwar Czechoslovakia* (New York: Columbia University Press, 1972); Lane and Kolankiewicz, *Social Groups in Polish Society;* Zdenek Strmiska, "Programme socialiste et rapports sociaux en U.R.S.S. et dans les pays socialistes," *Revue*

d'Etudes comparatives Est-Ouest 7, no. 3 (1976): 107-236; Zdenek Strmiska and Blanka Vaváková, "La stratification sociale de la société socialiste: À propos du livre de Pavel Machonin et des co-auteurs sur la stratification sociale dans la société tchecoslovaque," *Revue francaise de Sociologie* 13 (1972): 213-257; Alexander Matejko, *Social Change and Stratification in Eastern Europe* (New York: Praeger, 1974).

13. This process has been superbly documented in the works of H. Gordon Skilling, *Czechoslovakia's Interrupted Revolution;* Galia Golan, *The Czechoslovak Reform Movement: Communism in Crisis 1962-1968* (Cambridge: At the University Press, 1971); idem, *Reform Rule in Czechoslovakia: The Dubček Era 1968-1969* (Cambridge: At the University Press, 1973); and Vladimir V. Kusin, *Political Grouping in the Czechoslovak Reform Movement* (New York: Columbia University Press, 1972).

14. In an interesting study of dissent in Eastern Europe, Zygmunt Bauman argues that one of the important sources of dissent in socialist states results from clogged channels of upward mobility. See his "Social Dissent in the East European Political System," *Archives européennes de sociologie* 12 (1971): 25-51.

15. Jan Szczepański, *Polish Society* (New York: Random House, 1970), pp. 66-67. The Polish sociologist Jerzy Wiatr has also stated that there exist in Poland groups that are "with increasing frequency treated in the Polish literature as equivalent to interest groups functioning in the political systems of the capitalist countries." He argues that most of these groups operate through the formal official system and that "the Church, one could say, is the only 'opposition pressure group.'" "Elements of the Pluralism in the Polish Political System," *The Polish Sociological Bulletin*, no. 1 (1966), preprinted in the Polish Sociological Association, *Polish Sociology: Selection of Papers from The Polish Sociological Bulletin* (Wroclaw-Warsaw-Kraków-Gdánsk: Zaklad Narodowy imienia Ossolińskich, Wydawnictwo Polskiej Akademii Nauk, 1974), pp. 128-129. Finally, Georges Mond has also argued that "the Polish intellectuals have thus assumed the role of a pressure group. They try, in one way or another, to influence those in power and to participate in decision-making in socio-cultural, and even political matters." In Adam Bromke and John W. Strong, eds., *Gierek's Poland* (New York: Praeger, 1973), p. 130.

16. Thomas A. Baylis, *The Technical Intelligentsia and the East German Elite: Legitimacy and Social Change in Mature*

Communism (Berkeley-Los Angeles-London: University of California Press, 1974), p. 237.

17. See William F. Robinson, *The Pattern of Reform in Hungary* (New York: Praeger, 1973).

18. The process of "normalization" is clearly and succinctly described in Wlodzimierz Brus, *Socialist Ownership and Political Systems* (London-Boston: Routledge and Kegan Paul, 1975), pp. 141 ff. Brus argues that "in the USSR and the peoples' democracies not even partial political pluralism was permitted in the post-Stalin period. In all its basic elements the structure of actual relationships remained unchanged." However, in the light of his own discussion, I believe that it would be better to say that the pluralist tendencies that became so evident in 1956-1957 were gradually suppressed during the next decade.

19. Lane, "The Role of Social Groups," p. 312.

20. Ibid., pp. 312-313.

21. Cited in *Radio Free Europe Research, Situation Report, Poland*/25, October 13, 1977, p. 7. (Hereafter cited as *RFER, Poland*.) Although most issues of the *RFER, Poland* published since October 1976 have included articles on the activities of KOR, this issue has the most complete summary of its history.

22. Ibid.

23. Ibid., p. 8.

24. A large percentage of the one thousand active collaborators of KOR mentioned in May 1977 consisted of students. Three major petitions were submitted to the government calling for the "creation of a committee to investigate the truth of the allegations that workers of Radom and Ursus held by the police were beaten unconscious." These petitions were signed by 231 students in Gdańsk in February, 730 in Warsaw in March, and approximately 200 from the Catholic Univesity of Lublin. See *RFER, Poland*/8, March 16, 1977, pp. 3-4; *RFER, Poland*/13, May 30, 1977, p. 7.

25. *RFER, Poland*/16, June 15, 1977, pp. 1-2.

3. Eurocommunism and Innovation: A Western European Perspective*

Martin O. Heisler

During the past two years, the term *Eurocommunism* has come to denote the increasingly insistent and comprehensive assertions of independence of the most important nonruling communist parties in Europe. The leaders of especially the French, Italian, and more recently Spanish Communist parties (the PCF, PCI, and PCE) have progressively moved themselves, their organizations, policies, and world views away from the Communist Party of the Soviet Union (CPSU) and Soviet government.

These developments are very important for the Eurocommunist parties and the countries in which they operate, of course, since they are likely to change the political balance and perhaps the entire political ethos in those systems. But they also have substantial portent for Eastern Europe and the Soviet Union—indeed, for all communist parties and regimes.

Above all, Eurocommunism signals significant change. It reflects massive innovation inside the major communist parties of Western Europe and in the regimes of which they are parts; and it is likely to lead to even more sweeping changes in the coming years. It may also prove a source (threat?) of innovation for Eastern Europe and the Soviet

---
*See the editors' postscript on page 71.

Union internally, as well as for relations between them.

Most specialists have identified and analyzed Eurocommunism in terms of three traits.[1] First, it stresses the prerogatives of each national communist party to interpret and apply the tenets of Marxism-Leninism in its own way, appropriate to its own context. Second, Eurocommunist parties accept pluralist political models, in which political forces other than the party are accorded a continuing place. Thus, they are willing to forgo the stage of the "dictatorship of the proletariat" that suppresses all opposition. This is pluralism of sorts. It entails the acceptance of some important aspects of democracy and it influences both the strategy and the style of communist political action in the West. Third, since no European communist party in the West is likely to achieve an electoral majority in the foreseeable future, such parties tend to pursue power through coalitions with socialist and even moderate-to-conservative elements, aiming for popular or united fronts and more open, stable alliances with other political groups. This tendency, following largely from the contextual and pluralist concessions noted above, is exemplified by the PCI's movement toward "historic compromise" with Italy's Christian Democrats and by the development, since 1972, of a "common program" for political purposes by the PCF and the French Socialists.

This evolution of Western Europe's largest and most important communist parties represents attempts to legitimize or make widely acceptable the parties in societies that are still largely suspicious of them. These attempts are intended to show that these parties are quite independent of any external communist influences and, more or less like other parties, ready to play politics according to the accepted rules of the game. If such declarations of ideological and organizational autonomy portend genuine independence, they could eventually undermine Soviet influence in portions of Eastern Europe as well, since there is no reason to assume that the logic of Eurocommunism respects any particular geographic or ideological border. The domestic political aspects of Eurocommunism and its transnational, intra-(Soviet) bloc ramifications have serious implications for East-West relations also, especially in this "era of détente." For the Kissinger-Sonnenfeld doctrine evolved in the mid-1970s implied clearly demarcated spheres of control for the West and the Soviet Union. According to this doctrine, the West would recognize the Soviet Union's interests in Eastern Europe and would refrain from "destabilizing" or undermining areas within the Soviet sphere, with the hope that the Soviet Union would observe a similar hands-off attitude toward Western Europe. From this vantage point, the advances of Eurocommunism could be interpreted as intolerable communist penetration, particularly by those who do not accept as genuine the assertions of independence made by Eurocommunist parties. Indeed, this line of reasoning underlies much of the reflexive fear of and opposition to Eurocommunism. Conversely, the possibility that the Eurocommunist spirit will penetrate Eastern Europe may come to be regarded as a threat by the Soviet Union—a threat exported by the West.

Eurocommunism presents important and interesting problems at each of these three levels of analysis—the domestic, the intrabloc, and the East-West. Given the limits of space, most of this essay is devoted to the first of these. The discussion that follows concentrates on the nature of Eurocommunism and on why and how it might work to the advantage of the countries where it is most developed—and indirectly to the advantage of the Western Alliance. Ways of minimizing the risks associated with the entry of communist parties into the governments of democratic European societies will also be considered.

This emphasis is justified by a gap in the literature: few writers, especially in the United States, have gone beyond lamenting the prospect of communist participation in the national governments of major European states,[2] and there have been virtually no systematic assessments of the positive aspects of such participation or the means for controlling its dangers. Such assessments are essential, since blanket condemnation or helpless hand-wringing will in no way help to confront the challenges and opportunities of Eurocommunism.

II

From the perspective of domestic politics, there are three fundamental arguments in favor of the entry of communist parties into government in France, Italy, and Spain. First, it is often said that the absence of the communist parties will make extremely difficult—perhaps impossible—the effective government of Italy, meaningful political choice in France, and stability in Spain. Second, many Europeans, including steadfast noncommunists, aver that the extensive and long-lived electoral support of the PCF and PCI and the seemingly genuine appeal of the PCE to a not-negligible minority of Spanish voters have already provided them with a degree of legitimacy sufficient to make them respectable contenders for at least a share of power. The PCF's historic claims to represent a legitimate *French* political tradition,[3] the PCI's positive record in local and regional governments,[4] and all three Eurocommunist parties' convincing embrace of the European Community and willingness to accept NATO give credence to such views.

If the second argument militates against keeping the communist parties out of government in democratic regimes, the third can be considered a case in favor of drawing them in, especially when Western European countries are experiencing hard times and facing difficult, often unpopular, policy choices. In its simplest form, this argument is that communist parties should come to be associated by the electorate with some of the unpopular decisions and programs and some of the hardships and failures—such as austerity programs, inflation, unemployment, and civil disorder—that contemporary European governments may have to endure. In this way, the CPs could not cast blame on the political elements that carry responsibilities in these areas. Nor would they be able to imply that they could have done better.

These propositions can be examined comparatively. Since the circumstances in the three countries under consideration vary considerably, it seems advisable to proceed on a country-by-country basis, beginning with Italy, where the phenomenon of Eurocommunism seems the most extensively developed and the likeliest to lead to significant change in the near future.

It is clear that Italy continues to face a number of serious, simultaneous crises, especially the increasingly grave economic situation in both the public and private sectors; eroding trust in the political, economic, and even religious institutions of the society; and a growing polarization of ideological and cultural factions and regions. The Christian Democrats (DC), in power alone or as the dominant partner in coalitions, have governed for thirty years; and it has becoming increasingly evident that they can neither govern now nor fashion a stable coalition without the PCI.

The PCI is the next most important party in Italy. Not only does it have the second-largest electoral base after the DC—far ahead of third parties—but it has also established a generally positive record as the governing party of many of the country's largest and best-governed cities (most notably, Bologna). Since 1975, it has also assumed control of some of the new regional administrations and, to date, has acquitted itself well.

These are reasons for bringing the PCI into government, and the acute crisis faced by Italy militates in favor of doing so *now*. Co-opting the PCI at this time would not only improve the country's stability and, therefore, prospects for escaping its predicament, but would also associate the communists, in the minds of the public, with the difficult and often unpopular measures that will be required.

Even if it were so inclined (and its leaders for a generation have insisted with increasing vigor and credibility that it is not), the PCI would find it virtually impossible to establish control over a coalition it might enter. For, notwithstanding its electoral support and mass base and notwithstanding the recent demonstration of its ability to govern effectively and with respect for democratic norms at the local level, it is still distrusted by a substantial portion of the Italian population.[5] Thus, it is constrained in its actions and obsessed with establishing a democratic, moderate image.

At present, a strange "alliance of nondisruption" exists between the PCI and the DC. In return for being consulted by the tenuous DC government on most policy decisions, the PCI refrains from toppling the cabinet—something it could do almost at will. This is a form and degree of *co-optation:* by gaining access to the policymaking process (even if such access is informal and largely indirect), the PCI has gained a stake in the success of the regime. That stake or vested interest is, of course, proportional to the degree of access it receives in return for its cooperation; and the present arrangement is neither substantial enough nor adequately institutionalized to permit a positive prognosis.

As I have argued elsewhere at length, such co-optation has provided stable and effective government in other deeply divided European societies for decades.[6] It has been suggested that co-optation is in the interests of Eurocommunists as well as the current governing elements.[7]

The theory of co-optation suggests that the exchange of access to the policymaking process in return for regime-level support is most likely to produce stable and effective government when it has been in place from some time, routinized and legitimized. Although it remains to be seen whether such a strategy would be effective in other settings, it has much to recommend it in the Italian case. The current "alliance of nondisruption" can be regarded as a genuine innovation, which, if it can operate for a few years, may launch the institutionalized, legitimate co-optation of a Western communist party into a fundamentally democratic regime.

The French case differs substantially from the Italian, along several dimensions. Although France is not free of problems of governance and does not have as healthy an economy as it had from the mid-1950s through the mid-1970s, it clearly is not trapped in a downward spiral of the Italian variety.

Eurocommunism in France has focused on an electoral strategy aimed at gaining a majority in parliament and perhaps at capturing the presidency of the republic in tandem with the large and dynamic Socialist Party. Neither party has much prospect for achieving a majority alone in the near future, but in alliance with each other their chances appear promising.

Recognizing that the changes the Fifth Republic wrought in both the consitutional and party systems made success for either the Communists or the Socialists alone unlikely, the PCF and the Socialists experimented first with purely ad hoc electoral alliances and, then, as early as 1965, with more systematic and programmatic ties. This was a decade before the emergence of the Eurocommunist phenomenon.

But, for diverse reasons, the PCF's assertions of autonomy vis-à-vis the Soviet government and the CPSU, as well as its willingness to accommodate itself to a pluralist framework, were slower in developing and have remained somewhat more ambivalent than the PCI's. Recently, when the Gaullist-Giscardian coalition appeared most vulnerable less than six months before the legislative elections, the PCF decided to press its position regarding the scope of nationalization when (if) the coalition of the Left—the PCF, the Socialists of François Mitterrand, and the small Left Radical Movement—gained a parliamentary majority. And as this is being written, a few months before the legislative elections of 1978, the coalition of the Left—more than a decade in the building and more than five years after the drafting of the *"programme commun de gouvernement"* of the Socialists, PCF, and Left Radicals—is losing its popularity and its image as a workable alternative to the Center-Right, which has ruled for nearly two decades.

One of the fundamental differences between the PCI and the PCF is that the latter must compete with a large, well-organized, and dynamically led socialist party. The PCI, in contrast, is the only serious force on the Left in Italy. Another factor may be leadership at the top. The PCF's Georges Marchais lacks the intellectual depth, finesse, and popular appeal of the PCI's Enrico Berlinguer.

The PCF seems less able to operate effectively in a pluralist framework, and this weakness will make it more difficult for the party to gain a share of power. To the extent that the Socialists are able to capitalize on the general disenchantment of the French electorate with the Gaullists and their allies, they may well preempt the "serious," government-eligible segment of the left of the political spectrum. This would constrain the PCF to many more years in opposition.

Innovation through Eurocommunism in France, if it is to occur, will take the form of the development of a viable left-of-center political coalition—a counterweight to the right-of-center forces that have ruled the Fifth Republic. It could be argued that this modern-day version of the "Popular Front" of the 1930s will become truly innovative only if a coherent, integrated party of the Left emerges from the electoral alliances. Considering the difficulties experienced even in the loose frameworks attempted in the past decade and the organizational rigidities of both the PCF and the Socialists, this is not likely to occur.

The Spanish setting differs sharply from both the Italian and the French. First, during the forty years of the Franco regime, the Spanish Communist Party was outlawed, its leaders either in exile or underground, its organization virtually nonexistent, and its public image beyond the pale for the vast majority of the population. Second, as it emerged from four decades of oppression, it seemed well on the way toward becoming a major political force in the electoral arena, but in Spain's first free elections it failed to gain even 10 percent of the votes and seems destined to lag behind the Socialist Workers' Party, led by the highly attractive and able Felipe Gonzáles. Gonzáles, at thirty-five, offers a sharp contrast to the aging leadership of the PCE, many of whom spent the forty years of Franco's rule in exile in the Soviet Union or France and who consequently have had difficulty in establishing their credibility with the Spanish public.

The PCE's prospects are not particularly bright.[8] The new regime is presently governed by a center–moderate conservative coalition of fragmented political groups under the leadership of Adolfo Suárez. Should that government falter, the most likely replacement for it would be the Socialist Workers' Party and Gonzáles, since they garnered nearly 30 percent of the vote in the June 1977 elections (compared with 35 percent for Suárez's group). The PCE's poor third place, its relative lack of attractive, dynamic leaders, and the regional concentration of its electoral support (mostly in Catalonia)—all point to a long road ahead for the party.

The most important event in the PCE's months-old career in the open was the publication of Carrillo's *Eurocommunism and the State*. This book is generally considered to be the most comprehensive and vigorous attack on the Soviet Union from European communist quarters; and Carrillo was roundly attacked for it by the Soviet press shortly after the 1977 elections. Along with the more progressive elements in the party, he wears that condemnation as a badge of honor, but some of the old-line party members—including leaders who spent four decades in exile in Moscow—view it quite differently. Understandably, this has created friction within the party itself.

Spain's Eurocommunism, then, aside from Carrillo's tour de force, faces an uphill road to overcome the general suspicions of the Left that still prevail, namely, to develop a modern, progressive image and a coherent cadre. Likewise, it will be difficult to overcome the lead of the Socialist Workers' Party—either to displace it as the dominant force left of center or to make it dependent on an alliance with the PCE for victory. The prospects, as Meisler points out, are not bright.[9]

Eurocommunists stress the need to adapt communist doctrine and political practice to the setting in which a particular party operates, and our brief *tour d'horizon* of its three most important manifestations certainly bears out the importance of contextual factors. In Italy, Eurocommunism is likely to alter the nature not only of the communist phenomenon but also of the Italian regime itself. In France, if the electoral alliance and strategies of the PCF and Socialists succeed, the party system and the range of alternative governments will change substantially. In Spain, Eurocommunism may make the Spanish Communist Party respectable and may, in time, permit it a positive role in conjunction with more moderate elements on the left.

III

In all three countries, Eurocommunism has extended the range of political possibilities for forming governments. By asserting their independence from Moscow, stressing their willingness to play the political game according to democratic rules, and making themselves available for co-optation, Eurocommunist parties have changed communist practice in Western Europe and at the same time have altered prevailing political balances.

Questions remain, however, about the balance between potential threats from the active, positive involvement of communist parties in the governance of democratic regimes and the possible benefits that might flow from such participation. The Soviet dissident Andrei Amalrik, for instance, has expressed great trepidation.[10] He voiced the fears of many who believe that once communist parties gain a place in the governments of Western democracies, they will revert to type: that is, they will subvert their allies and opponents and blatantly disregard democratic political practices.

This possibility cannot be ruled out completely. However, at some juncture the practices as well as words of Eurocommunists must be judged without preconceptions. In addition, the alternatives to according responsible roles to communist parties in some European systems need to be considered. One alternative to opening the doors to legalized communist participation is to continue governing troubled regimes with narrowly based and consequently often ineffective governments. This poses the real risk of collapse, particularly in Italy. Such a collapse might be followed by a massive turn toward extremism—including dictatorship either from the Right or the Left. Under such circumstances, the PCI might consider itself endowed with a mandate to "save the country." Its entry into the government under such circumstances—not entirely far-fetched—would surely be less appealing than its co-optation into a coalition dominated by the DC.

It is difficult to accept the suggestion, often made by those who oppose a Eurocommunist entry into government, that a communist party acting as a junior partner in a coalition— the French and Spanish systems come to mind—will tend to undermine its allies. Such a takeover would have to be spaced over several years in all of the countries in question. During that period several elections would be held, and other checks on the CPs could be exerted. Furthermore, such fears ignore the continuing *embourgeoisement* of communist cadres—a process that is likely to be accelerated once the party enters into a governing role.

Amalrik and others tend to assume that communist parties

in such systems as France and Italy will be able to manage their coalition partners with ease. There is little evidence for this view. On the contrary, the record of both the French socialists and the DC in Italy—as well as the promise of the Socialist Workers' Party in Spain—suggest the contrary. At the very least, this assumption must be examined case by case and kept current through analyses of prevailing organizational, situational, and personality considerations.

In sum, Eurocommunism signifies change in the communist parties of several major European countries, in relationships between national parties and the Soviet Union, and perhaps most important, in the regimes of the countries in which these parties operate. Its form and importance vary from country to country, but Eurocommunism bears careful watching for the foreseeable future—in both Western and Eastern Europe, and in its long-term ramifications, even in the Soviet Union.

Notes

1. See, for instance, Charles Gati, "The 'Europeanization' of Communism?" *Foreign Affairs* 55, no. 3 (April 1977): 539-553; and Kevin Devlin, "The Challenge of Eurocommunism," *Problems of Communism* 26, no. 1 (January-February 1977): 1-20.

2. The most notable exception is Professor Peter Lange of Harvard University. In a number of papers he explores the phenomenon in great depth. See in particular his "Notes on the PCI and Possible Outcomes of Italy's Crisis" (Paper prepared for the Seminar on the Italian Crisis, Turin, Fondazione Luigi Einaudi, March, 1977); and his "Report on the State Department Sponsored Conference on 'Eurocommunism and Regional Institutions'" (Airlie House, Virginia, May, 1977). Unfortunately, limits of space do not permit me to reflect the richness of Professor Lange's descriptions and analyses. See also Donald L. M. Blackmer and Sidney Tarrow, eds., *Communism in Italy and France* (Princeton, N.J.: Princeton University Press, 1975).

3. Ronald Tiersky, *French Communism: 1920-1970* (New York: Columbia University Press, 1974); Annie Kriegel, ed. *Le Congrès de Tours*, décembre 1920; *naissance du Parti communiste*

français (Paris: Julliard, 1964).

4. Ina Lee Selden, "Italy's Communists Practicing Power," *New York Times*, July 31, 1977, provides an excellent survey.

5. Lange, "Notes on the PCI," pp. 37*ff.*

6. Martin O. Heisler, *Politics in Europe: Structures and Processes in Some Postindustrial Democracies* (New York: David McKay, 1974), Chapter 2.

7. Gati, "The 'Europeanization' of Communism?" p. 553.

8. Stanley Meisler, "Spain's New Democracy," *Foreign Affairs* 56, no. 1 (October 1977): 199-200.

9. Ibid.

10. *International Herald Tribune*, June 21, 1977, p. 4.

Postscript

Chapter 3 was completed in the Fall of 1977; this postscript was written on March 20, 1978, the day after the second round of the French legislative elections, and a week after the Italan Christian Democrats and the PCI concluded a new, historic agreement.

The failure of the Socialist-Communist electoral alliance to unseat the Gaullist-Giscardian majority can be largely attributed to the dogmatism and belated cooperation of the PCF with is Socialist allies. The Center-Right capitalized on the radical stance of the PCF in the campaign; also many Socialist voters, reacting to the PCF's doctrinaire positions, supported the candidates of the governing coalition instead of Communists in sufficient numbers to permit the Center-Right to carry the day.

In Italy, the relationship between the DC and the PCI was tightened substantially, bringing the latter further into the mainstream of the country's political life. A few months back, the PCI agreed to abstain from parliamentary votes in which the minority DC cabinet's viability was threatened, but in early March it agreed to vote with the Government. In return, the PCI gained increased access to policymaking, and although it still has no cabinet positions, that possibility now seems real and not too distant.

—*The Editors*

Part 2
Diffusion of Innovation across Systems

4. Yugoslav Self-Management and Its Influence on Other Socialist States

Gary K. Bertsch

Identifying the diffusion of innovations from one political unit to another is a difficult task even under ideal research conditions. Doing it in more closed systems where ideology makes any political change a highly sensitive matter, such as in the communist states we are concerned with here, is even more difficult. Attempting to assess the diffusion of an innovation from a sometimes "outcast" or so-called revisionist state such as Yugoslavia to an "orthodox" communist state such as the Soviet Union is almost impossible. Even if the Soviet Union were vitally interested in a particular Yugoslav innovation and even if it were in fact adopting certain aspects of the innovation, the Soviet leaders would probably attempt to disguise the innovation's origins for ideological reasons. To admit that there is something to learn from a state one has ostracized over the years is something that proud leaders are unlikely to do.

Yet there is a reason to believe that Yugoslavia has had an impact upon the states of the socialist community, including the Soviet Union. With the possible exception of some of the Asian communist states, Yugoslavia is clearly the most innovative within the current array of communist states. If we conceive of an innovation as the development and implementation of a new program that is institutionalized and generally acknowledged to have systemic effects, it is clear that a number of far-reaching experiments in Yugoslavia can be viewed as innovations.[1] I would include here the foreign policy of nonalignment, the economic system based upon market socialism, and the far-reaching system of industrial democracy called self-management. All have become institutionalized and have clearly affected the Yugoslav sociopolitical system.

This last innovation, that of industrial democracy, is an extremely critical issue in socialist and Marxist thought. Lenin contended that socialism would not be successful and communism would not be achieved unless full democracy was implemented. Yet the records of most of his successors in promoting democratic development have been far from impressive. Although most leaders have articulated democratic ideals and principles, their policies have either instituted or preserved centralized and authoritarian systems of rule. Few have pursued innovative policies conducive to democratic development. Clearly, none have achieved the level of democracy implicit in Marxist theory.

Yugoslavia, however, is a partial exception to the general communist pattern of centralized, authoritarian rule. Over the last few decades, the Yugoslav leaders have articulated, designed, and done much to implement a complex system of "self-managing socialism." Self-managing socialism is based upon direct democratic decision making in the policy process through assemblies of voters drawn from local communities, enterprises, and sociopolitical organizations. In my mind, the Yugoslav self-management system can be considered an innovation in the communist world because of the unprecedented decision-making power and autonomy it has given to individuals and groups within social, political, and economic organizations. This chapter will take a closer look at the Yugoslav innovation of self-management and the nature of its diffusion to other communist states.

Why Was Self-Management Initiated?

Self-management in Yugoslavia resulted from a crisis. Following their expulsion from the Cominform and their break with Stalinism, the Yugoslav leaders began to reexamine Marxist and Leninist theory to determine—stated in simplistic terms—what had gone wrong with Soviet ideology. The idea of self-management was purportedly first raised by Milovan Djilas, shared with members of the inner circle within the Politburo (Tito was apparently excluded at this point), and discussed with union leaders and other officials. Shortly thereafter, the idea was shared with Tito, supported, and made into law. The primary piece of legislation, the Basic Law on the Management of State Economic Enterprises and Higher Economic Associations by Work Collectives, was approved by the National Assembly on June 27, 1950. Although this act, generally known as the law on workers' self-management, was at least as much a propaganda strategy to distinguish the Yugoslav system from the bureaucratic and etatist features of the Soviet system as it was a genuine effort to democratize the system, it set in motion a chain of events that carried Yugoslavia far in the direction of industrial democracy.

Before 1950, Yugoslavia adhered to the orthodox communist model of centralized management and administration. After the legislation of the early 1950s, an initial period of cautious experimentation took place. At this phase of Yugoslav development, two models of socialist administration—that is, state socialism and self-managing socialism—coexisted, and, as one might expect, created considerable structural confusion and role ambiguities.

In the 1960s the Yugoslav leaders attempted to move far beyond the conventional model of state socialism. Major efforts were made to further decentralize and democratize organizational life and the federal state system in general. Economic organizations were made the basic units of production, decision making, planning, and administration. This critical innovation in the administration of economic life was undertaken in order to give workers greater control over the administration of their work. Although the reformers hoped this system would have benefits in the areas of worker motivation, production, and efficiency, no reliable research assessed the effects of these reforms during this early period. Within the federal system, republics and provinces assumed greater control over their internal affairs, a move that resulted in a more open, decentralized, and democratic system.

The early 1970s, however, witnessed a return to party dominance and a recentralization of power within federal governmental and party organs. As a result of increasing regional conflict and nationalism and as a result of the central party leaders' feeling that they were increasingly powerless to deal with these difficulties, the central League of Communists (LCY) organization moved to reassume its leading role in the early 1970s and to end the trend toward regional decentralization and particularism. During the same period, however, major efforts were made to increase still further mass involvement in industrial and organizational decision making. For example, the 1974 constitution includes several refinements that decentralize decision making power to "basic work units" (BWU) and provides workers' councils at all levels of autonomous work.

By the mid-1970s, the self-management system had resulted in a high level of institutionalization. The first prerequisite of an innovation, institutionalization, has certainly been fulfilled. Today, the Yugoslavs have a highly developed and formal system of industrial and organizational democracy within a moderately centralized federal political system.

Has Self-Management Had Systemic Effects?

In order to qualify as a genuine innovation, self-management must do more than appear in the constitution, in the speeches of leaders, and in the charters and bylaws of organizations. It must also affect the behavior of individuals and the way the system operates. Among other things, self-management was intended to democratize organizational life. If it has, then it has had at least one important systemic effect.

In order to address this question, we must review the relevant empirical research on the impact of self-management on participation and influence in decision making processes.[2] A critical review of the considerable research on the question indicates that self-management has had both successes and failures.[3] Some research calls attention to the considerable discrepancy between the ideal of direct democracy and the way Yugoslav organizations are really run,[4] yet most observers call attention to the considerable progress that the Yugoslavs have made in democratic development.[5]

In addition, cross-national comparisons present Yugoslavia in a particularly favorable light. The five-nation study of Tannenbaum et al. shows that both Yugoslav workers and managers perceive higher levels of organizational democracy in their own firms than their counterparts in Austria, Italy, Israel, or the United States perceive in theirs.[6] Not only did the Yugoslavs perceive higher levels of organizational democracy in their own firms, but they also preferred it.

David Granick's study of Rumania, the GDR, Hungary, and Yugoslavia also places the Yugoslavs in a favorable light and provides further evidence that the self-management system has had systemic effects. In fact, Granick concludes that self-management is the one factor that most distinguishes Yugoslavia's industrial system from that of the

COMECON countries.[7]

Self-management has also had effects on Yugoslav society. The ideology of self-managing socialism brought about some dissolution of powers within central party and governmental structures. Decreasing power at the national level coincided with a rise in the influence of a growing technology and regional leadership. Although the LCY's reassertion of party dominance in the early 1970s diminished the power of these sectors, Yugoslav society has been changed. A considerable body of sociological and anthropological research attests to the fact that Yugoslavia has moved toward a more active participant political culture. This and most other available research allows us to conclude that the self-management system has resulted in a higher level of democratization in organizational and social life.[8]

Costs and Benefits to the Innovators

It is reasonable to assume that potential adopters of an innovation will take into account the experience of the innovators in deciding whether to adopt a particular innovation. Accordingly, what costs and benefits have been incurred by the Yugoslavs? Is their record attractive to potential adopters?

Ideologically speaking, self-management has produced considerable benefits. When expelled from the Cominform, Yugoslavia needed a strong and powerful issue to separate and distinguish itself from the bureaucratized, etatist Soviet form of socialism. Self-management and citizen participation became the centerpiece of Yugoslav ideology. Self-management meaningfully connects democracy and socialism and puts power in the hands of those to whom the ideology says it rightly belongs. If it were pursued to its logical conclusion, self-management could become the guiding framework for a genuinely democratic and humanistic ideology, something far more in line with classical Marxism than state socialism.[9]

At the same time, the idea of self-management confronts the Yugoslav leaders with a serious ideological dilemma. How can one pursue self-management to its logical conclusion and simultaneously maintain a centralized, one-party state? How can the people really manage their own affairs when they find the party interfering in their constitutionally guaranteed areas of decision making autonomy? In a sense, this is an ideological cost of the self-management system, one with which the leaders find it very difficult to deal.[10]

Economically speaking, the innovation indicates a mixed record in Yugoslavia. In terms of costs, self-management has been at least partly responsible for high unemployment, high emigration, high inflation, a heavy negative balance of trade, duplicative investment, increasing social and regional inequalities, and difficulties in coordinating investments among regions and enterprises. Of course, some of these difficulties resulted from factors in addition to or apart from the self-management system. Inflationary pressures, for example, have stemmed more from the policy of maintaining high rates of investment and growth than from efforts by the self-managed enterprises to increase personal income payments. Yet potential adopters would have to be somewhat chary of adoption in view of Yugoslavia's numerous economic difficulties, which are at least partially attributable to a decentralized, self-managed system.

To some extent, these economic costs are offset by benefits. Real gross domestic product has grown at about 6 percent per year since the mid 1950s, and per capita income in constant prices has increased by about two and a half times during the same period. The World Bank Economic Report on Yugoslavia concludes that development has been characterized by rapid structural change, a fairly high rate of employment growth, and, particularly since 1965, a rapid growth of output per worker and rising standards of living.[11]

In the sociopolitical realm, the balance appears to be

clearly on the side of benefits. Three major achievements appear to stand out. First is the unquestionable movement toward greater industrial and participatory democracy. Although certain cynics and critics scoff at shortcomings and difficulties in the system, the large majority of the population supports the basic values and goals underlying self-management. Within this favorable setting, an increasing percentage of the population is participating in public life and exercising some influence over the choice of public policies and the conditions of their work. Second, self-management has tended to slow the bureaucratization and excessive centralization of sociopolitical and economic life. In stemming what seems elsewhere to be a technological imperative, the system has displayed itself as a surprisingly powerful force. An important consequence of this effort to decentralize organizational power has been to challenge such disturbing trends as increased alienation, apathy, and other unfortunate characteristics of industrial and postindustrial life. Third, the emphasis on industrial democracy has been a strong humanizing force within Yugoslavia. All observers would agree that Yugoslavia has made considerable progress in developing "socialism with a human face." This achievement, it seems to me, is a clear benefit for a state seriously involved in the construction of communism, and it is largely attributable to advances in the self-management realm.

Yugoslav and other proponents of self-management would like to believe that the benefits of their experiment in industrial democracy clearly outweigh the costs. From the perspective of most nonpartisan observers, the weighing of costs and benefits is extremely complex, and the overall picture is still unclear. To the prospective adopters in the socialist community, the costs, particularly ideological costs, are quite heavy. Yet there is considerable interest in the Yugoslav experiment. As we will see, however, diffusion of political innovations in the socialist community is not based upon a rational choice model. Because of several crucial factors, the adoption of even the most attractive innovations is not dependent upon a simple weighing of costs and benefits.

Diffusion of Self-Management

Before an innovation is diffused, it must be communicated. Accordingly, it is instructive to consider the possible channels of communication and the use of these channels before attempting to assess the diffusion or lack of diffusion of self-management in other communist states. One possible channel by which self-management principles and procedures might be exported involves scholarly contacts. To what extent do Yugoslav scholars disseminate information on the theory and practice of self-management, and to what extent are scholars from other communist states willing or able to receive it? One good indicator of information exchange of this kind is participation in international conferences and symposia. In 1972 the First International Conference on Participation and Self-Management was held at the Inter-University Centre for Postgraduate Studies in Dubrovnik, Yugoslavia. Full delegations were invited from the Soviet Union and European communist states. Over two hundred participants gathered from across the globe. Yet the official list of participants indicates that there was only one representative from the Soviet Union, one from Hungary, and three from Poland. The Second International Conference on the same topic—held in Paris in 1977—resulted in a similar lack of exchange. Although there is evidence that considerably more information is communicated among scholars through less formal channels, it is fair to say that the amount of information exchanged through scholarly contacts is considerably less than what could be exchanged.

Another channel through which information about the self-management innovation is communicated is governmental contacts. Tito's visit to China in 1977 was used, among other things, to exchange information about the two social systems. Upon Tito's return, Chinese officials told foreign journalists they were studying the Yugoslav system with the expectation that some elements might be adopted for Chinese use. One element drawing particular attention appears to be self-management, as Chinese leaders seek to increase worker motivation, efficiency, and output. Whether the Chinese are in fact seriously considering the Yugoslav system or simply attempting to flatter Tito is a point of speculation. However, we can conclude with some certainty that considerable information was and is being exchanged through official, governmental channels and could at some point conceivably result in some kind of diffusion.

There have been other exchanges of governmental officials for the purpose of exploring the theory, practice, and relevance of self-management. Polish officials went to Yugoslavia in 1956, a Czechoslovak delegation was sent in the mid-1960s, and Khrushchev indicated that an official Soviet delegation would be sent while he was visiting Yugoslavia in 1963.

Scholarly journals such as *Sociologija* or *Nase Teme,* political or ideological journals such as *Socialist Thought and Practice,* and newspapers such as *Politika* and *Borba* are perhaps the major sources by which information on self-management is disseminated to other communist states. Many scientific and governmental organizations in East European countries and the Soviet Union subscribe to these periodicals and follow them with considerable interest.

Although such channels as those described above are utilized, surprisingly little is known about Yugoslav self-management. Perhaps the most highly informed sector in these societies are small groups within the scientific and scholarly communities. On the basis of evidence provided by certain Yugoslav scholars, small groups of East European scholars maintain rather close contact with their Yugoslav counterparts. Although these scholars are well informed, few have any real influence upon policymaking within their countries. Hence, their knowledge of the intricacies of the Yugoslav innovation has little impact upon the diffusion process. Occasionally, however, they report their knowledge in periodicals, which can place the issues of workers' councils, communal assemblies, and industrial democracy on the public agenda. In this way, they can have some influence on party officials and government administrators. Individuals in government agencies and the bureaucracy appear to have only the most general knowledge of self-management—really only impressions—and their opinions tend to correspond with the official party opinion. This suggests that they are aware of what their leaders officially pronounce about the innovation but that they have studied little original materials for themselves. Within the high political leadership, within the central committees and above, there appears to be considerable diversity in the level of information and knowledge of the Yugoslav system. Although some officials appear to be surprisingly well informed, particularly those who are more highly educated and from technocratic backgrounds, the majority hold everything from vague, ideologically based impressions to assorted facts and misinformation that they have gleaned from scientific and intelligence reports and from personal conversations and experience.

Finally, the general public in Eastern Europe is very poorly informed about the self-management system and other innovations in Yugoslavia. Relying on the mass media for information, it periodically gets general reports on the "political situation in Yugoslavia." These reports vary in their objectivity across the different states and according to the nature of foreign relations with Yugoslavia. They almost never report on self-management in sufficient depth and specificity to provide the interested reader with the information necessary to judge self-management's relevance to his own life, work organization, or society.

Evidence of Diffusion

There has been no wholesale adoption of the Yugoslav self-management system in any communist state and very little diffusion of various elements thereof. Some states have experimented with certain components of the system, and others have made daring, but short-lived, adoptions; but the general picture is that of minimal diffusion. In commenting on the influence of Yugoslav self-management (and peasant farming) upon the Soviet Union, Smolinski notes not only that has there been no appreciable influence, but also that "one is hard put to find any evidence of a serious interest in these pathbreaking innovations, or any analytical studies . . . of their theoretical significance and importance."[12]

Although it is impossible to make the link, there is considerable experimentation and change in the East European countries in the areas of administrative reorganization and decentralization of decision making powers. These changes could conceivably be linked to the Yugoslav innovation. For example, there is the devaluation of central authority within the GDR involving consultative organs, brigades of socialist labor, work and research collectives, and various social and economic control bodies.[13] Of course, the closest GDR analogues to the Yugoslav workers' councils—the workers' committees of 1956-1957 and the production committees—are now both defunct. Whether these earlier experiments or the more recent changes can be attributed to the Yugoslav experiment is debatable, but it seems reasonable to contend that at the very least, the Yugoslav experience provided ideas and guidance.

Hungarian reforms, including the creation of general assemblies of workers and economic committees, the shift of central controls over enterprises from an individualized physical planning control base to a financial planning base, and the shift of central control over enterprises from branch ministries to interministerial committees, may in some cases have borrowed from the Yugoslav experience. As Kanet notes, "Recent developments in Hungary . . . seemed to be modeled in part on the changes in Yugoslavia, although, to date, they have been far more restricted.[14] Gitelman contends that the Hungarians might even have gone so far as to create workers' councils once again, but that they refrained from doing so because of their unhappy experience with them in 1956 and because they wanted to avoid rousing Soviet fears that they were flirting with the Yugoslav model.[15] To my knowledge, there is no evidence that the Hungarian innovators have ever had any intention of making the enterprise the primary unit of decision making activity as it is in the Yugoslav system. Although the far-reaching Hungarian reforms may have been in part influenced by Yugoslavia, the Hungarians have done their best to avoid association with the Yugoslav model and to avoid having any of their reforms viewed as ideological challenges to the Soviet model. The fact that they have instituted the most innovative and far-reaching reforms among the COMECON countries may attest to their success in this regard.

The Czechoslovak reforms in 1968 seem to have been heavily influenced by the Yugoslav experience. In the area of party policy, the 1968 Czechoslovak new draft statutes seemed to correspond rather closely with those of the LCY. For example, the statutes provided for a time limit for holding office, a curb on the power of professional party employees, attempts to preclude the accumulation of excessive power in the hands of any one person, the federalization of the party, and so on. In the area of workers' participation and management, the *Action Program* showed a democratic and technocratic flavor that closely paralleled Yugoslav ideology, including the creation of workers' councils, attacks on income "leveling" and excessive egalitarianism, and so forth. Giving these councils the right to appoint the enterprise director and to participate in many policy decisions appears to borrow directly from the

Yugoslav system. The swiftness and decisiveness of the Soviet intervention clearly indicated their fear of permitting the unfettered diffusion of integral elements of the Yugoslav model. In areas of ideological sensitivity, the Soviets have shown little tolerance for diffusion of "unorthodox" ideas and practice.

Apart from the ill-fated Czechoslovak experience, the most significant examples of diffusion and adoption of the Yugoslav model appear to have come in areas that tend toward greater administrative and ideological neutrality. Consider, for example, the pure and simple decentralization of decision making authority. Here we might include the GDR's New Economic System and its efforts to decentralize decision making power. As long as the East Germans' intention was to rationalize and make a highly managed economy more efficient, the changes were tolerated, but if they came to threaten the highly centralized leadership of the system, as the reform movement in Czechoslovakia ultimately did, they would have overstepped the bounds of permissibility.

Other areas tending toward neutrality include the decentralization of investment decisions and increasing concerns with efficiency and profitability. Hungarian reforms in decentralizing more investment decisions to the enterprise level, for example, have copied the Yugoslav pattern. There also appears to be a growing feeling in the East European states that efficiency will be best promoted if decisions are guided by a maximum return on capital. Although these are important changes, none challenge the basic tenets of Soviet ideology.

I have not attempted to systematically identify and quantify all cases of the diffusion and adoption of various elements of the Yugoslav self-management model within the socialist community. However, on the basis of my study, I have determined that there have been cases where the adoption of basic elements of the Yugoslav model seems rather clear. In some, the innovations were adopted, institutionalized, and performed well within the system. In others, such as Czechoslovkia in 1968, what appeared to be rather major adoptions of the Yugoslav model were attempted but then aborted. Now we will consider the factors that seem to determine these patterns of diffusion and adoption.

Explaining Rates of Diffusion and Adoption

The Perceptions and Behavior of the Soviet Leaders

The most critical factor explaining the rates of diffusion and adoption of the Yugoslav innovation within East European states appears to be the perceptions and behavior of the Soviet leaders. We must ask, therefore, to what degree do Soviet leaders perceive self-management, or elements thereof, as being consistent with past Soviet experience, current Soviet ideology, and future needs within the socialist community. As Samuel Sharp observed in his survey of Soviet criticisms of Yugoslav self-management, "Soviet evaluations have been consistently negative with the exception of a brief period during Khrushchev's tenure when the Soviet leader showed a rather positive interest in the experiment and even may have toyed with the notion of applying it in the Soviet Union itself."[16] Although the current leaders show an occasional sign of tolerance, the general feeling is negative. The negative appraisals reached a peak in the aftermath of the Czechoslovak affair, when the Soviet leaders warned regularly of the dangers of reducing the central government's role in planning, of replacing it with a market mechanism, and of moving toward full autonomy of enterprises. The question of self-management is still too politicized to be compatible with Soviet ideology, basically because the Yugoslav model is viewed as an alternative, competitive model of socialism with the following unacceptable features: (1) a diminished role for the party, (2) a market economy, (3) too little central planning.

Soviet leaders also perceive the Yugoslav system to have far more costs than benefits, both for themselves and for other East European countries. The Soviets contend and apparently sincerely believe that autonomous enterprises simply do not have the technological information and expertise to make choices in the interests of the broader community. Sharp concludes his analysis of Soviet criticisms by noting: "The most frequently repeated point is that the transfer of management to workers' collectives does not constitute an advance over the system of state ownership which in the Soviet Union is the prevalent system of public ownership of the means of production."[17]

Finally, the Soviet leaders have a deep fear of the sort of wholesale adoption of the Yugoslav model they perceived to be unfolding in Czechoslovakia in 1968. At the same time, they appear to be cautiously willing to allow other states (Hungary, Poland, and the GDR) to experiment with decentralization and some elements of market socialism on a more limited basis. The cardinal principle seems to be the leading role of the party. Experiments with decentralization, worker participation, and forms of participatory democracy will be permitted as long as they do not challenge the orthodox Soviet ideology and the leading roles of the ruling parties.

The Perceptions and Behaviors of National Elites

The national leaders' perceptions of the compatibility, relative advantage, and experimentation with innovations are of major importance in explaining their interest in, and adoption of, elements of the Yugoslav model. The leaders in all countries uniformly believe that the Yugoslav model in its entirety is unacceptable. In their minds, the expansion of workers' participation can not be allowed to inhibit the leading roles of the party and state organs, something that wholesale adoption of the model might do. Nor can it be allowed to bring about the dismantling of the central planning and command systems. However, though the overall model is off limits, various elements of self-management—administrative "deconcentration," worker participation in decision making, and so forth—are in some cases considered acceptable.

Many East European leaders have viewed the relative advantage of self-management rather differently from their Soviet counterparts. In those cases where worker participation, including workers' councils, have been pursued the farthest, the leaders obviously reasoned that the advantages outweighed the costs. The history of Soviet interventions in these cases (Hungary 1956, Poland 1956, Czechoslovakia 1968) clearly indicates that the Soviets did not agree with their reasoning.

The apparent interest of the new post-Mao Chinese leadership in the Yugoslav model suggests that assessments of the costs and benefits of an innovation, or of its compatibility with the existing ideology, may change with time or the passing of a powerful leader. It is still too early to assess the seriousness of Chinese interest in experimenting with the self-management system, but the fact that they are now publicly declaring their interest in the system after a long period of hostile denunciations is quite remarkable in itself. The apparent change in attitudes in China testifies to the importance of the national leadership's attitudes and perceptions in explaining patterns of diffusion and adoption.

The recent East German, Hungarian, and Polish experiences testify to the different leadership perceptions regarding "trialability" and their feelings that various components of self-management can be experimented with on a limited basis. Although the Soviet leaders appear to avoid adopting any aspects of the model for fear that it cannot be experimented without resulting in unwanted changes in other parts of the system, the East Germans, Hungarians, and Poles are interested in elements of the model that bring administrative reorganization and decentralization, certain aspects of market socialism, and expanded citizen involvement without adopting the whole system.

The reform movements in these East European states, whether or not they were directly influenced by the Yugoslav experience, indicate that the leaders in these countries have perceived the questions of compatibility, relative advantage, and "trialability" differently from the Soviets. As a result, they have been more open to change in the direction of the Yugoslav model than have their counterparts in the USSR. In the absence of Soviet dominance, a question we will consider below, the diffusion and adoption of elements of the Yugoslav model would doubtlessly have been much greater.

Structure of Influence Relationships

Another important factor explaining the diffusion and adoption of innovations within communist states is the structure of influence relationships among the concerned parties. Within the East European community, it is no secret that the Soviets play the role of "gatekeepers." Considerable research has shown that opinion leaders tend to act as gatekeepers to prevent innovations with which they disagree and at times to promote those that are unlikely to change the structure of the existing system. The Soviet leaders assumed the role of gatekeepers and intervened in Czechoslovakia in 1968; elsewhere, they permitted the reforms in Hungary because of their different perceptions of the end results of the two reform movements. As R. V. Burks notes in his study of technology and political change in East Europe, the decision on the type of reform the East Europeans decide to institute appears to rest in Moscow.[18]

The structure of influence relationships within the socialist community has been marked by restricted communication channels. Before a Yugoslav innovation can be carefully studied and considered for possible adoption, it must be fully communicated. East European elites and scholars have often been reluctant to communicate with the Yugoslavs on this question for fear of "guilt by association."

Finally, this situation and other correlates of the influence relationships in the socialist community impair the rationality of the decision processes concerning this highly politicized issue of innovation and change. It is simply unrealistic to apply rational actor models to the diffusion process in East Europe and predict that diffusion will occur when benefits of the innovation outweigh the costs. As Gitelman has noted, the socialist community is a highly uncertain system where the rules of rational decision making do not always apply. What may be a rational adoption of the Yugoslav self-management model in one system may be overruled for political and ideological considerations held by leaders in the USSR.

Changes in Patterns of Diffusion and Adoption?

Could any factors or future developments result in higher rates of diffusion and adoption of self-management among the states of the socialist community? Since the Soviet leadership is the most critical factor in determining diffusion and adoption patterns in East Europe, any changes in the leadership could have major implications. An intriguing possibility is that leadership change in the USSR that might result in different interpretations of the questions of compatibility, relative advantage, and "trialability." If the forces of Soviet democratization are as strong as some observers suggest[19] and if there is indeed a trend toward pragmatism and problem solving at the expense of prescriptive ideology,[20] then future Soviet leaders might take points of view that would be viewed internally and externally as no more revolutionary than the post-Stalin leadership in the Soviet Union and the post-Mao leadership in China. New Soviet leaders could contend that there is nothing particularly incompatible between Yugoslav self-management and Soviet ideology. This point of view is even more persuasive in view of the reassertion of the LCY's leading role in 1970 and the "return to orthodoxy" in other important respects.

Different Soviet priorities and changes in the cost/benefit ratio might also change perceptions of relative advantage. More emphasis on such explicitly Marxist concepts as humanization, participation, and socialist democracy could easily tip the balance. If there were a leadership change in the USSR and if perceptions and ideological emphases changed as described, the Soviet leaders could use the successful Hungarian, Polish, and East German trials of partial adoption as justifications for moving one step further. Under such circumstances, the diffusion and adoption of the self-management innovation could unfold rather quickly.

Leadership changes, greater confidence in European security, and a more stable international system could result in a restructuring of the present influence relationships and in a loosening of Soviet control over innovations in East European states. The chances of this appear unlikely in the short run, yet they should not be ruled out for the longer term.

Although sociopolitical and economic crises in the Soviet Union and East European states may bring a heavier emphasis upon administrative centralization and ideological orthodoxy, they could also bring a more pragmatic and receptive posture on self-management. If the present Soviet emphasis on quality and efficiency does not result in the expected and needed improvement in the economic system over the next five or ten years, new methods for promoting worker motivation will be considered. The Yugoslav self-management system appears to be one of the more logical alternatives. This possibility would be even more likely if Yugoslavia were to record significant economic and sociopolitical advances over the next decade. Although the present situation does not augur well for major Yugoslav breakthroughs, advances will be closely evaluated by the Soviets and East Europeans and affect their choices concerning innovation and change.

Another possible development in Yugoslavia could make the socialist community more receptive to the self-management innovation, namely, the possibility of a Yugoslav return to orthodoxy in foreign and domestic policy areas apart from that of self-management. Soviet concern with Yugoslav policy in the past has always focused more on nonalignment, market socialism, and the role of the party than it has on self-management. If the Yugoslavs were to assume more orthodox positions in the 1970s in respect to the leading role of the LCY—the self-management innovation would not seem nearly as threatening.

A final development could also change the nature of diffusion patterns involving self-management. If there are both a depoliticization of the self-management question and an increased emphasis on pragmatism and problem solving, the self-management innovation will be considered more on its own merits and less on the basis of prescriptive ideology. If this and any one or more developments occur simultaneously, the likelihood for interest in and adoption of elements of the self-management system would increase exponentially.

If these contingencies led to the diffusion and adoption of the self-management innovation in the Soviet Union, East European, and other communist states, what would be the impact upon these systems? There seems to be no reason, first of all, why the structural prerequisites—workers' councils, communal assemblies, and so forth—cannot be established within these diverse settings. In fact, they (or similar variations) already exist in most of the countries. The major question is whether they would be permitted to function in the way they are intended to. If they were given meaningful decision making power and autonomy and if they were institutionalized within the system, they would necessitate a major restructuring of some important dimensions of these societies' political cultures. The self-management innovation requires political values, beliefs, and attitudes that are participatory and democratic. These may be difficult to develop in a one-party state with a highly centralized formal power structure, as the Yugoslav experience clearly indicates. However, the Yugoslav experiment also indicates that social self-management, industrial democracy, and one-party rule can coexist. Although the arrangement may not be optional and although the party may occasionally interfere in decisions reserved in principle for the workers, the system may still be an advancement over the orthodox administrative hierarchy.

Summary and Conclusion

The Yugoslav system of workers' self-management is obviously one of the most significant innovations in communist states. However, with the partial exceptions of some ill-fated and aborted adoptions in certain states and selective adoption in certain ideologically neutral areas in these and other states, the diffusion of the Yugoslav experiment has not been extensive. Although past leaders have tended to perceive extensive incompatibility, the relative disadvantages of self-management, and the indivisibility of the innovation, and although they were often constrained by the structure of influence relationships in the socialist community, the pattern could change in the future. A variety of future contingencies, some more likely than others, could result, particularly if they occur in some combination, in much higher rates of diffusion.

Perhaps the most interesting observation is not that the Yugoslav innovation of self-management has had relatively little effect upon other communist states, but rather that it has had some effect and that it could, under certain conditions, have a much greater effect in the future. The future is particularly interesting if we imagine an alternative diffusion system in the socialist community, a system that is characterized by new leaders who are less security conscious, less politicized, and more pragmatic. Under such a system, national leaders could search more rationally for answers to the needs and challenges of contemporary socialist life and, in so doing, view the Yugoslav system on the basis of its true costs and benefits. If this were done, a much higher rate of diffusion and adoption would doubtlessly take place.

Notes

1. This conception of an innovation is taken from Zvi Y. Gitelman, "The Diffusion of Innovation: From Eastern Europe to the Soviet Union," in *The Influence of Eastern Europe and the Soviet West on the USSR*, ed. Roman Szporluk (New York: Praeger, 1975), p. 17.

2. See the papers presented at the First International Conference on Participation and Self-Management in 1972 and published in six volumes as *Participation and Self-Management* (Zagreb: Institute for Social Research, 1972). For more recent views, see the papers presented at the Second International Conference on Participation and Self-Management in Paris, September 1977.

3. G. David Garson, *On Democratic Administration and Socialist Self-Management: A Comparative Survey Emphasizing the Yugoslav Experiment*, Sage Professional Papers in Administrative and Policy Studies, vol. 2, series no. 03-015 (Beverly Hills and London: Sage Publications, 1975).

4. See Joso Gorciar, "Workers Self-Management: Ideal Type and Social Reality," *Participation and Self-Management*, 1: 18-32; Gary Bertsch and Josip Obradović, "Ideals and Reality: An Analysis of Influence in Twenty Yugoslav Firms," in *Participation, Workers' Control, and Self-Management*, ed. William Dunn (Pittsburgh: University of Pittsburgh Press, forthcoming).

5. This conclusion can be drawn from the considerable research conducted by scholars from many countries and presented at both the First and Second International Conferences on Participation and Self-Management.

6. Arnold S. Tannenbaum et al., *Hierarchy in Organizations* (San Francisco: Jossey Bass Publishers, 1974).

7. David Granick, *Enterprise Guidance in Eastern Europe* (Princeton, N.J.: Princeton University Press, 1975).

8. Several books attest to this trend, including Bogdan Denis Denitch, *The Legitimation of a Revolution* (New Haven and London: Yale University Press, 1976); Dennison Rusinow, *The Yugoslav Experiment 1948-1974* (Berkeley and Los Angeles: University of California Press, 1977).

9. For a consideration of the philosophical and ideological issues, see Branko Horvat, Mihailo Markovic, and Rudi Supek, *Self-Governing Socialism*, vol. 1 (White Plains, N.Y.: International Arts and Sciences Press, 1975).

10. For a statement by the leaders, see *Ideological and Political Offensive of the League of Communists of Yugoslavia* (Belgrade: Secretariat for Information, 1972).

11. *Yugoslavia: Development with Decentralization* (Baltimore and London: Johns Hopkins University Press, 1975), p. 3.

12. Leon Smolinski, "East European Influences on Soviet Economic Thought and Reforms," in Szporluk, *The Influence of Eastern Europe and the Soviet West on the USSR*, p. 75.

13. Thomas A. Baylis, "Socialist Democracy in the Workplace: The Orthodox and Self-Management Models," in *Authoritarian Politics in Communist Europe*, ed. Andrew C. Janos (Berkeley: Institute of International Studies, 1976), p. 129.

14. Roger E. Kanet, "Modernizing Interaction Within Eastern Europe," in *The Politics of Modernization in Eastern Europe*, ed. Charles Gati (New York: Praeger, 1974), p. 291.

15. Gitelman, "The Diffusion of Political Innovation."

16. Samuel Sharp, "The Yugoslav Experiment in Self-Management: Soviet Criticisms," *Studies in Comparative Communism* 4 (July-October 1971): 169.

17. Sharp, "The Yugoslav Experiment," p. 171.

18. R. V. Burks, "Technology and Political Change in Eastern Europe," in *Change in Communist Systems*, ed. Chalmers Johnson (Stanford, Calif.: Stanford University Press, 1970).

19. Jerry F. Hough, "The Brezhnev Era: The Man and the System," *Problems of Communism* 25, no. 2 (1976): 1-17; and idem, "Political Participation in the Soviet Union," *Soviet Studies* 28, no. 1 (1976): 3-20.

20. William A. Welsh, "Policy Science as an Innovative Area in Socialist Systems," Chapter 1 in this volume.

5. Problems Facing the Yugoslav Communist Movement: A Comment

R. V. Burks

Our appraisal of the problems facing the League of Communists (LCY) must be determined by an understanding of the following background forces and factors.

The Croatian crisis of 1971 resulted in a vigorous effort to reassert the leading role of the LCY. This reversal of policy, however, proved difficult to implement. The most fundamental obstacle to the new policy was the decay of party discipline, a weakness inextricably linked to the spread of interest groups. However, the republic parties also tend to dominate the decision making process within the LCY itself, so that it proved impossible to recreate a single decision making center for the regime as a whole. The court of last resort, therefore, continues to be Tito's villa on Brioni, where a variety of institutions and interests are represented in irregular summit meetings in which interest aggregation —to use the jargon of the political scientist—takes final place, and the Yugoslav marshal serves as the ultimate arbiter.

For the future of Yugoslavia, it is doubtful that the LCY will be able to recover its leading role or reestablish a single

These remarks were originally formulated at a conference on "Yugoslavia: Accomplishments and Problems," held at the Woodrow Wilson Center, Smithsonian Institution, in October 1977.

decision making center: the pluralization of Yugoslav society is probably irreversible. The best that can be hoped for is a situation of *contrived ambiguity* in which the LCY pretends to play the leading role but in fact shares power with the republic parties, the federal system, and the institutions of worker self-management. The requirement for the success of contrived ambiguity is the continued absence of ideological controversy and of the factional struggle that is its inevitable accompaniment.

One should attack the paradox of contemporary Yugoslavia or the desirability of a resolution of the problem of power by placing at the center of the discussion the following question: why cannot the process of pluralization be permitted to reach its logical conclusion safely?

The answers to this question tell us much about the nature of the East European communist regimes in general. Measured on the Western scale, Yugoslavia is a poor country, a fact that is in itself a destabilizing force, and its scanty resources are unevenly distributed. The difference between the living standards in the north and the living standards in the south is striking, although this difference may no longer be growing. There are in fact two Yugoslavias, one lying north of the Danube, Sava, and Kupa rivers, but also including metropolitan Belgrade, the other lying south of that line. Northern Yugoslavia is a part of Central Europe; southern Yugoslavia belongs to the darkest Balkans. The nearest analogy is provided by neighboring Italy, where a pluralist society labors from one crisis to the next and would probably collapse except for its inclusion in the Common Market.

Yugoslavia's problem is worse than Italy's, to be sure, since in Yugoslavia the division into wealthier and poorer halves roughly parallels a separation along ethnic, or national, lines. Thus if pluralism were allowed to achieve its full expression, the Croats, who firmly believe that their standard of living would be markedly higher were they free of the Yugoslav south, might well opt for an independent national existence. At the same time, Kosovo might seek union with Albania proper, and Macedonia could come to gravitate in the orbit of Sofia, whose foreign policy has long been predicated on the assumption that the Yugoslav federation would ultimately come apart at the seams.

Yugoslavia has an additional problem characteristic of the European socialist states generally. Large elements of the Yugoslav elite, including the party apparatus, are basically ambivalent in their attitude toward the new socialist order. But this ambivalence was also made clear by the inability of the Croatian party to grapple with the problem of *Matica Hrvatska* when that long-established cultural organization underwent a sudden metamorphosis in 1971, becoming almost overnight a national opposition party preparing the way for ultimate independence. Croatia in 1971 experienced the beginning of a political landslide, roughly comparable to that which Czechoslovakia had begun to undergo three years earlier.

In my view, the Yugoslav regime still has not reached the harbor of legitimacy, although it is appreciably closer to that blessed port than any of its fellows. Despite the fact that Yugoslav society has undergone the most far-reaching pluralization that any socialist regime has ever experienced, the LCY could probably not put together a majority in a free election.

On this score there is some evidence. Opinion polls taken among Hungarians traveling in Western Europe in 1976-77 ($N = 1,368$) and among Rumanian visitors to that area ($N = 1,254$) revealed that in hypothetical free elections only 5 percent of Hungarian voters, and 11 per cent of the Rumanians, would vote the communist ticket. To my knowledge, no such poll has yet been conducted among Yugoslav visitors to the West, but I would think the Hungarian and Rumanian results would indicate an order of magnitude no greater than, say, 20 percent.

Additional evidence can be found in a little-noticed reversal of Yugoslav policy. In the 1960s it appeared as though the LCY was experimenting with semifree elections. What could be a more effective step toward the illusive state of legitimation than elections in which the voter had a real choice, not between parties to be sure (since that might involve unacceptable risk), but between candidates? As long as there was such choice, Yugoslav parliamentary life was worth following. But the incipient political landslide in Croatia, and its impact in places such as Slovenia and Kosovo, led the Yugoslav leadership to the distasteful conclusion that even semifree elections were out of the question.

The constitution of 1974, therefore, introduced a system of indirect election, in which each legislature was composed of delegates chosen by the legislative bodies below it. In addition, at each level either a third chamber or a special delegation was introduced, selected either by the party itself or by one of its various transmission belts, such as the Socialist Alliance. The crisis of 1971 had revealed to the Yugoslav leadership the true state of public opinion!

That the LCY is itself asking these questions may be inferred from the legislative system established by the constitution of 1974 as well as from the new institutions of social compacts and self-management agreements. It is not practicable, in my view, for the delegates at each legislative level to refer back to the delegations that chose them for instruction on each and every issue; nor do I believe that delegates who continue their ordinary jobs can function independently. Experience with the social compacts and the self-management agreements, none of which are enforceable in the regular courts of law, already suggests that they will with great difficulty reach across republic boundaries or combine a wealthy enterprise with a poor one. I suspect these systems were in part designed to make LCY more necessary than it has been in the past.

At a more fundamental level, there are the confederal elements in the new constitution, such as the provision that makes federal revenue heavily dependent upon annual grants provided by the parliaments of the republics. Surely the operation of the federal government, which has been reduced to an apparatus for achieving agreement among the republics, will depend on the filling of the interstices between the republics by the LCY.

Besides giving the LCY a greater role, the creators of the new institutions evidently also have in mind the pervasive and still unsolved problem of legitimation. The new institutions are intended to replace, if we may use the words of Kardelj, the "political pluralism of the classical parliamentary system" with the "pluralism of self-management interests."

More than that, they are intended to attack head-on the problem of elite ambivalence. The discipline and the drive of a Leninist party are not possible without a set of doctrines to believe in, an ideology, a religious faith. In the heroic days of Partisan warfare, the ideology was in fact an all-inclusive Yugoslav nationalism, one purified and made feasible by a social order of justice and equality, an order to be erected in the postwar era on the principles of Marxism-Leninism-Stalinism. Today and for the future, the ideology of the LCY is that of the federal, or the confederal, association of different and distinct nations in a society made just and equitable by that same "pluralism of self-management interests."

The LCY must somehow convince its peoples that this is an acceptable substitute for "the political pluralism of the classical parliamentary system." But more importantly, it must convince the elites of the pragmatic validity of the new ideology, that it can hold the country together and bring it forward into an age of greater economic productivity and political stability.

We ask a final question. Suppose the LCY should fail in its efforts to uphold its "contrived ambiguity" and fall victim to the disintegrative impact of pluralization. Is any alternative cement available to be applied to the masonry of the federation?

The alternative, if there is one, is to be found in the People's Army. For the first time in the history of communism, the army has been given a position constitutionally anchored in the political life of a socialist state, having its allotted quota of representatives in the central party bodies. In the bargain, army leaders have at one time or another been given control of such political resources as the security police and the domestic air lines.

The officers of the People's Army, from NCO through the rank of colonel, are preponderantly Serbian and Montenegrin, drawn, therefore, from peoples who traditionally have identified their fortunes with those of the Yugoslav state. It was Tito's implicit threat that he would occupy the Croatian Republic with this army that brought the crisis of 1971 to its close. The Croats believed that Tito would carry out his threat, in contrast to the Czechs and Slovaks, who did not believe Brezhnev would carry out his.

But I would venture to assert that in Tito's mind the People's Army represents a fallback position, a maneuver of last resort. In the East European socialist world, a military dictatorship is without precedent, so the future of such an enterprise is difficult to foresee. But it does not seem reasonable to believe that the People's Army could manage Yugoslavia's complex problems better than the LCY. On the contrary.

6. Two Germanies and the Transformation of Europe

John M. Starrels

The emergence of domestic terrorism in West Germany and the sudden appearance of "domestic" political dissent in East Germany are two reflections of one common phenomenon: the challenge each German regime faces in its attempt to grapple with unplanned, and partially uncontrollable, change. This chapter will briefly examine how change is handled within the context of intra-German association.

At the outset, it is important to state what will *not* be attempted. No effort is made to document the various transformations that have taken place in the realm of intra-German relations from the late 1940s to the late 1970s. Nor is there an effort to evaluate the specific policies that are prominently associated with the Brandt-Bahr conception of intra-German relations, contained in the Basic Treaty of 1973.[1] Rather, those basic themes are chosen for examination, themes that reflect upon the present, and perhaps even the future, conduct of relations between West and East Germany. First, we will examine the relevance of "Eurocommunism" for East and West Germany's specialized competition; heavier emphasis is placed on the GDR's response to Eurocommunism if only because the evolution of a more tolerant form of Marxism-Leninism in southern Europe poses more direct, and potentially more serious, challenges to East Germany's system of one-party authority than it does for the Federal Republic. Second, we examine the timeliness of human rights issues within the context of intra-German relations; in this instance, the concern is directed at elite and nonelite dissent within the German Democratic Republic and at the ways in which those developments are simultaneously associated with the West German policy of reunification toward East Germany. And, *finally*, we make some observations on the meaning of "national' development within East Germany as it relates to the evolution of mobilized socialism in Europe as a whole.

Germany and Eurocommunism

Both German systems have been powerfully influenced by transnational movements in European politics. Fascism reached its ultimate expression in the Third Reich, and parliamentary government in Germany was ultimately destroyed by the pitched confrontations between adherents of communism and National Socialism during the latter years of the Weimar Republic. At the end of World War II, the triumph of Soviet-style communism in East Germany set the stage for future ideological thinking in the German Democratic Republic (GDR)—particularly the regime's response to "Third Way" doctrine, which has become prominently associated with various proponents of Eurocommunism today. In West Germany, the ideological evolution of East Germany, the splintered history of German social democracy, and the restorationist appeals of Christian democracy combined to defeat the possibility of ideological-mass politics in the Federal Republic.

The evolution of seemingly independent communist parties in Western Europe has had an impact on the conduct of intra-German relations. For the Federal Republic, Eurocommunism has certainly introduced yet another element of complexity to the question of how Western Europe is ultimately going to evolve. One is advised to recall that West Germany's embrace of supranational integration during the immediate postwar period was based on a strong commitment to a noncommunist alternative for Western Europe as a whole. And today, even with a nominally Social Democratic regime now in power, the Federal Republic continues to represent the anticommunist and anti-Leftist trends in Western European politics. But in terms of the German Democratic Republic, Eurocommunism has come to serve West German purposes, which specifically relate to Bonn's ongoing criticism of one-party authoritarianism in East Germany. From this vantage point, Santiago Carrillo's criticism of the Soviet Union and the one-party regimes of Eastern Europe can be fitted into the more specific West German criticism of political monopoly in the GDR. Within the specialized context of intra-German affairs, Eurocommunism represents yet another cosmopolitanizing force the Federal Republic can use in its attempt to open up East Germany to larger patterns of multilateral change.

Not surprisingly, East Germany confronts and defines the Eurocommunist issue from a different vantage point.[2] For its ruling communist party, the Socialist Unity Party (SED), the emergence of increasingly self-confident and highly nationalistic parties in Western Europe has come to pose a variety of painful questions, if not actual dilemmas, for the regime. Clearly, the SED, along with the Soviet Union, has been consistently favorable to parties that style themselves along the ideological lines of Marxism-Leninism. Western analyses of Soviet and Eastern European reactions to the evolution of Eurocommunism in Western Europe occasionally betray a sense of hopeful thinking. Indeed, the Soviet Union, given a monopolistic interpretation of its role in the international communist movement, may feel threatened by the development of increasingly nationalistic counterpart organizations in southern Europe; but this hardly justifies the argument that the USSR, or the GDR, is dead set against the emergence of a Marxist-Leninist regime in Western Europe. For East Germany, nonetheless, the emergence of a new brand of "liberalism" within the framework of a Marxist-Leninist organization poses several troubling questions for the SED.

First, the challenge put forward by Marchais, Carrillo, and Berlinguer reawakens an older struggle that has been going on in the German Left for at least a century. For the SED, the issue becomes one of reconciling the competing claims of so-called *revolutionary* vs. *reformatory* Marxists, of reconciling the positions held by Eduard Bernstein and Willy Brandt (among others) and the nonpluralistic views of Lenin and Walter Ulbricht. If the proclamations of the Italian or Spanish parties are to be taken at face value—a question on its own merits, which deserves serious research—communism, or some form of "advanced" socialism, can evolve within the framework of existing parliamentary institutions; after a socialist party, or a constellation of parties, comes to power, peaceful, i.e., nonviolent, transformations will continue to occur. If this argument is taken seriously, what challenges does it pose to the kind of authority the SED exercised in its part of Germany? Not only does the liberal strand of Eurocommunism directly challenge the SED's claims of legitimacy for the present and the future, but it also places serious question marks around the original motivations that guided East Germany's orthodox communists in their quest for power at the end of World War II. Because historical legitimization has been so important in the SED's search for legitimacy, challenges emanating from an historical interpretation of its earlier evolution should not be ignored or underemphasized.

Second, and more specifically, the Eurocommunist question cannot be and is not divorced from the ongoing debate between the West German SPD and the East German SED. The Honecker regime's strong embrace of the proletarian elements of Marxism-Leninism is yet another attempt to differentiate its brand of socialism from the less intense version of social democracy that has come to power in the Federal Republic. And though party statements rarely betray the existence of oppositional elements within the SED itself, one can assume that the SED's attack on revisionism in West German social democracy is no less directed at groups within its own society who are not committed to the postulates and practices of orthodox German communism within the GDR. Certainly, it was far easier for the East German regime to generate continuous polemics against the "revanchist" policies of the CDU/CSU when the CDU/CSU was in power in the Federal Republic. But it has become extraordinarily difficult for the SED to mount a similar offensive against an ideological counterpart such as the SPD—the classic enemy. To the degree that the SED finds itself uneasy when it confronts the more open, and explicitly more pluralistic, views of a Berlinguer or Carrillo, to that same extent does Eurocommunism reawaken a complex series of older arguments that pit East German communism against West German "reform" socialism.

Finally, one of the more fascinating questions relevant to East Germany's response to Eurocommunism has to do with the impact of such thinking on the consciousness of average GDR citizens. The celebrated meeting of European Marxist parties in East Berlin in June 1976 brought in its wake a startling emergence of disagreement between the French and Italian parties and their more orthodox authoritarian allies in Eastern Europe. That the official SED daily *Neues Deutschland* printed the complete texts of these discussions is worthy of attention in this regard.[3] But what kinds of influences do disagreements between Eastern and Western European communist parties exert on the broad population within East Germany? Certainly, there is room for honest speculation on a subject of this nature. But when Santiago Carrillo or Enrique Berlinguer begin to question the general applicability of the Soviet developmental model for other European countries, and given the excessive degree to which the SED has attempted to legitimize itself within East Germany through an almost complete borrowing of Soviet organizational and ideological principles, there is good reason to assume that the broad population might also question the developmental profile that the SED has chosen to adopt for the GDR.

Human Rights and the SED

The emergence of a human rights movement in the GDR is, in one sense, surprising. The SED has been able to engineer its own, albeit more modest, "German economic miracle." The standard of living in East Germany continues to be the highest in the Soviet bloc. On the international front, the GDR has achieved worldwide recognition. And yet—and perhaps even because of these above transformations—the human rights movement in East Germany is very much alive. But why now? Several obvious considerations deserve brief mention here.

First, the Final Act of the Helsinki Conference has introduced an unwelcome complexity to discussions taking place in Eastern Europe and the Soviet Union on the meaning of civil rights and the obligations and rights of contemporary citizenship. The impact of this document has been of some significance to the GDR as well.

Second, even though the SED has gradually relaxed its harsh policies of social control and mass mobilization since the late 1950s, heavy elements of authoritarianism remain in the GDR. The Helsinki document, in and of itself, is not responsible for the upsurge of popular and elite dissatisfaction with the positions taken by their regime on the rights of individuals, the legitimacy of organized group life "outside" the strict confines of SED control, and the theoretical "right" of all individuals—including loyal communists—to travel outside the borders of the GDR wherever their personal whims might take them. Indeed, as the average East German becomes increasingly affluent, the desire to travel to the West will probably increase. The growth of a consumption-oriented society in the German Democratic Republic may—over the long term—be the most important element in the extension of human rights in that society. From this vantage point, the Helsinki document only legitimizes existing currents of popular and elite dissatisfaction in the GDR.

Finally, what has been the impact of intra-German entente on the human rights movement in East Germany? Certain obvious points are significant here. In the largest sense, the existence of a competitive German alternative has always—since the end of World War II—stimulated a latent dissatisfaction in East Germany. During the 1950s, the Federal Republic's dramatic economic gains, its relative independence, and the relative impoverishment of East Germany's economy tended to accentuate the pull of West Germany on the population of the GDR. The Berlin Wall and an imposing border fortification system (which simultaneously splits the two parts of Germany and the two parts of Berlin from each other) have not dulled the attractiveness of the Federal Republic; they have transformed it. Individuals and groups may not be able to escape to West Berlin or West Germany with the relative ease that was once possible, but they can easily see evidence of how their life compares with life in the Federal Republic. East Germany can be reached by West German radio and TV, a reality that has introduced a de facto element of pluralism within the GDR.

But the real transformation in East German life vis-à-vis the Federal Republic has come in the institutional and psychological aftermath of the Basic Treaty. This complex series of protocols and agreements cuts across an imposing range of policy areas, from provisions for medical aid given to nationals of the other country, to long-run economic and financial accords ("the German Swing") that tie the two systems together in an expanding pattern of specialized independence. Each policy element of the Treaty is important unto itself, but certainly the arrangements that allow West Germans and Berliners to travel to the GDR is the most dramatic example of what intra-German entente can bring. In 1976 alone, 8 million West Germans visited East Germany.

But what do these considerations have to do with the evolution of a human rights movement in the German Democratic Republic? In part, the expansion of intra-German contact only solidifies the potential for increased West German influence in East German life; this "constant" in the German national equation nonetheless suggests that dissent in East Germany is given powerful symbolic and material support by the Federal Republic. In an increasingly affluent and self-confident society, the costs of dissent tend to decrease in any event, but the competitive model of West Germany undoubtedly represents an important source of psychological support for individuals in the GDR who want to change things in their own society or who wish to transfer allegiance to "another" part of Germany itself.

"National" Development

An understanding of the competitive relationship of an intra-German entente must include an awareness that the two Germanies are typical of advanced industrial societies more generally. This recognition does not rob a discussion of intra-German dynamics of the exclusively "German," or national, element, which forms an integral part of that analysis. The question, however, is one of determining the most appropriate framework for an understanding of that dynamic. In my view, that framework is based on the realization that the two Germanies are no longer (assuming they ever really were) "interchangeable pieces." Although they still share a variety of commonalities, including the same language and a relatively comparable standard of living, these two systems are in many ways radically different from each other. And yet they are no less representative of broad-scale processes in which ideology, industrialization, the growth of mass consumerism, and the parallel upsurge of individual demands for self-realization play important roles in national development.

The importance of emphasizing both the commonalities and differences reflected in intra-German relations is brought home in examinations that reach beyond the special future awaiting the two Germanies: hence, the significance of Eurocommunism, the Helsinki and Belgrade meetings, strategic arms limitation talks (SALT), and multiple force reduction (MFR) for the European future as a whole. But once again, the singular approaches taken by the two German states need not—and indeed should not—be submerged within the specialized contexts of German history and the evolution of the two systems over the past thirty years. For what we seem to be talking about, ultimately, in any examination of intra-German relations is the long-term future of Europe itself. From this vantage point, the study of West Germany's engagement with East Germany is no less a specialized examination of how Europe as a whole might also evolve.[4]

These observations have a special relevance for the future potential of mobilized socialism in Western Europe and for the East German response to the challenge of Eurocommunism. Two concluding points seem especially pertinent here. First, Eurocommunism challenges the SED's claim to historical legitimacy, its ongoing attempt to legitimize its form of politics within the developmental circumstances of postwar Eastern Europe. Did East Germany's communist leaders have to suppress social democrats and other forms of political expression in order to build socialism in the GDR? Even though domestic Marxist-Leninist regimes in Eastern Europe can and do defend their historical paths by relating twists and turns in party ideology to the "special" circumstances posed within their own societies, communism is—necessarily and ultimately—a universalistic doctrine. It is so for the SED no less than it is so for the Soviet Union or the PCI. But, secondly, if the challenges posed by the more liberal elements of Western European communism have occasionally unnerved the SED, the regime no less presides over one of the most successful and fascinating elements of Marxist-Leninist development in European and world politics. And even though serious questions need to be raised about the exercise of political authority within the German Democratic Republic, its proximity to Western Europe makes the SED one of the inevitable points of contrast if a counterpart organization in the West finds itself on the threshold of power.

Notes

1. Consult two sources on this subject: Peter Christian Ludz, *Die DDR zwischen Ost und West* (Munich: C. H. Beck, 1977), pp. 242-318; *Die Entwicklung der Beziehungen zwischen der Bundesrepublik Deutchsland und der Deutschen Demokratischen Republic* (Ministry for Inner-German Relations, Bonn, 1977)

2. See Heinz Timmermann's short piece on this subject, "Carrillo, Moskau und die SED," *Deutschland Archiv* 10, no. 8 (August 1977): 789-794.

3. For an examination of that event, see Karl Wilhelm Frick, "Die SED und die europäishe KP-Konferenz," *Deutschland Archiv* 9, no. 7 (July 1976): 673-677.

4. See John Starrels, "Comparative and Elite Politics," *World Politics* 29, no. 1 (October 1976): 139-142, for some general observations on the "comparative" dimension of German politics vis-à-vis the two Germanies, and particularly the GDR.

7. The Impact of Eurocommunism on the Socialist Community

Joan Barth Urban

In the wake of the Conference of European Communist and Workers' Parties held in East Berlin in June 1976, Eurocommunism emerged as a subject of controversy among noncommunist observers and communist polemicists alike. In the West, some observers interpreted it as a tactical ruse designed to further the cause of Soviet-style communism. Others saw it as portending the final conversion of Western communism to democratic socialism. A corollary of the latter, rather optimistic, view was that the democratization of communism in West Europe would, for example, undermine the tenuous legitimacy of the orthodox communist party-states in East Europe. The reform communists in Italy and Spain, even France, would somehow join forces with the political dissidents in Czechoslovakia, Poland, and elsewhere to bring about "socialism with a human face" in the Soviet bloc.

This chapter will treat the Eurocommunist phenomenon in a less hyperbolic and more systematic manner. The first section will differentiate Eurocommunism—as defined by its proponents—from the other major variants of European communism. The second section will suggest an analytical framework that may shed light on the limits as well as the possibilities of Eurocommunist influence within the socialist community. To be more precise, I hope to provide a conceptual basis for the following hypothesis: as long as the Eurocommunists remain bona fide members of the international communist movement, they will enhance the leverage and maneuverability of the more reform-minded Soviet bloc leadership groups vis-à-vis their more orthodox comrades. The conclusion will support this hypothesis with some illustrations from recent political developments within the European communist movement.

"Eurocommunism" and the Communist Parties of Europe

Proponents of Eurocommunism define it in terms of the following concepts: constitutionalism, pluralism, and regionalism. They argue, first of all, that Eurocommunism seeks to transform capitalism into socialism by legal means within the existing constitutional order. It aims to persuade the overwhelming majority of the electorate of the virtues of socialism while moving toward this goal by gradual steps, each of which is taken only on the basis of broad popular consensus. As a corollary, the Eurocommunists concede that a legal and peaceful revolution can be achieved only through communist cooperation with other socialist-oriented political groups and that such cooperation entails compromise as well as competition. With regard to the second key concept—pluralism—Eurocommunist spokesmen envisage a socialist society in which political and philosophical diversity will remain legitimate. The prosocialist parties (communist included) that come to comprise the bulk of voters during the revolutionary process will continue to compete in the electoral arena under socialism, alternating in power according to majority will. Moreover, given the ideological differences among the socialist competitors, the state will perforce assume a "lay" character, countenancing a wide range of philosophical views in civil society. Finally, the Eurocommunists argue that the Western communist parties have common interests and goals that may lend themselves to regional coordination. They also reject any form of international communist organizational structure, including, since the 1976 Berlin meeting, global or continental conferences designed to hammer out joint programmatic declarations. At the same time, they favor harmonious ties with *all* communist parties in addition to multilateral consultations and cooperation among parties with common problems and outlooks.

In its ideal form, Eurocommunism is thus the antithesis of communism as practiced by the ruling CPs in the socialist community. Soviet spokesmen eschew regionalism as contrary to, if not subversive of, proletarian internationalism, which Moscow defines as the voluntary subordination of national party interests to the interests of the movement as a whole. Soviet-style socialism also decries pluralism as contrary to, if not subversive of, the "leading role of the communist party," which Moscow deems a "general law" of socialist development binding on all CPs. Furthermore, Soviet ideologues are skeptical, even hostile, toward the notion of a constitutional transition to socialism, arguing (much as the Chinese did during the heyday of Sino-Soviet polemics in the 1960s) that the bourgeoisie has never peacefully acquiesced in its own demise.

But how does this profile of Eurocommunism compare to reality? The four major West European communist parties—the French (PCF), Italian (PCI), Portuguese (PCP), and Spanish (PCE)—may be said to represent diverse points on a spectrum only one pole of which approximates the Eurocommunist position. Closest to that pole are the Italian and Spanish CPs, whose programmatic declarations embrace by and large the profile of Eurocommunism sketched out above. The PCI and PCE have professed their commitment to a pluralist form of socialist society at least since the Warsaw Pact invasion of Czechoslovakia in 1968 and have rejected not only the Soviet model but also the very notion of "general laws" of socialist construction. They have, to date, given evidence of good faith in pursuing a legal, consensual, evolutionary transition to socialism. Since the June 1976 parliamentary elections in Italy, when the PCI vote for the Chamber of Deputies jumped from its 1972 high of 27.2 percent to 34.4 percent, the Italian Communists have followed a policy of cooperation and compromise with the minority Christian Democratic government of Premier Giulio Andreotti. Despite rank-and-file restiveness over its cautious line, the Berlinguer leadership negotiated a joint legislative program with the Christian Democrats and smaller center-left parties in the spring of 1977. The Spanish Communists, during the parliamentary elections of June 1977, took a position actually to the right of the larger Socialist Workers' Party, even accepting as their own the colors of the Spanish monarchy. On questions relating to inter-CP ties, the PCI and PCE practice what they preach. They have consistently condemned the Soviet invasion of Czechoslovakia, taken a conciliatory approach toward Peking, rejected "proletarian internationalism" as defined by Moscow, and urged regional consultations and coordination among West European CPs.

By way of contrast, the Portuguese Communist Party stands at the opposite pole of the West European communist spectrum. During the Portuguese crisis of mid-1975, PCP leader Alvaro Cunhal made headlines with his contempt for Western parliamentarianism and praise for the Soviet model of socialism. His party's abortive effort to gain power through political manipulation and intimidation elicited public condemnation by both the PCI and the PCE. With regard to international communist ties, the Portuguese party supported the Warsaw Pact invasion of Prague, has opposed overtures to Peking, hails Soviet-style proletarian internationalism, and keeps its distance from the movement toward Western CP regionalism.

In recent years the French Communist Party has taken an

equivocal position on all the questions noted above: the strategy of revolution, the character of socialism, and the principles of interparty relations. To be sure, since 1956 the PCF has paid lip service to the possibility of a parliamentary path to power. More recently, the signing of the Common Program with the French Socialists and Left Radicals in 1972 seemed to lend substance to that posture. Yet at the same time the French CP has tended to favor competition over compromise in dealing with its left-wing allies, especially because the balance of power within the Union of the Left shifted toward the Socialists. The Communists' vituperation toward the Socialists at the Twenty-First PCF Congress in October 1974 (on the heels of François Mitterrand's near victory in the 1974 presidential contest) and their intransigence during the mid-1977 negotiations for a renewal of the Common Program are cases in point. Such conduct suggests that the PCF's approach to the Union of the Left has more in common with the popular-front goal of the 1930s, i.e., communist hegemony, than with the principle of interparty parity.

The PCF's slogan of "socialism in French colors" is equally ambiguous. The party leadership repudiated the concept of "the dictatorship of the proletariat" with great fanfare at the Twenty-Second PCF Congress in February 1976; yet in his report to that congress, Georges Marchais reaffirmed his party's commitment to "general laws" of socialist construction, including the leading role of the communist party under socialism. By the same token, in late 1975 *l'Humanité* began to denounce Soviet treatment of political dissidents; yet the PCF refrained from the systematic and systemic criticism of Soviet bloc regimes that appeared in the Italian and Spanish communist press.[1] On questions of interparty relations, the French CP has perhaps been least equivocal. In the winter of 1976 it began insisting that the observance of proletarian internationalism entailed "reciprocal solidarity," i.e., Moscow's support for the policies of non-Soviet CPs as well as vice versa. The specific bone of contention was the Brezhnev regime's maintenance of cordial relations with the Élysée despite the Union of the Left's growing strength and prospects for victory. From November 1975, moreover, the PCF began to gravitate toward a regional entente with the PCI and PCE, with Marchais publicly accepting the label *Eurocommunist* at the tripartite Madrid summit of March 1977.

The Impact of Eurocommunism: A Conceptual Framework

There has been much speculation in the West on the possible impact of the Western CPs on the Soviet bloc or, conversely, on the likelihood of a rupture along the lines of the Sino-Soviet dispute between Moscow and, say, the PCI or PCE. At the same time, little attention is devoted to differentiating the issues in dispute between Moscow and Peking, on the one hand, and between Moscow and the Eurocommunists on the other. In a nutshell, the Sino-Soviet dispute does not involve basic principles. The intensity of their ideological polemics notwithstanding, the Chinese and Soviet CPs have never disagreed on the need for communist leadership under socialism, on the desirability of communist hegemony during the revolutionary process, or even on the premise that imperialism is inherently aggressive. They have simply accused each other of departing from these principles. On a theoretical level, therefore, the differences between Eurocommunism and Soviet communism are far more profound than the differences between China and the Soviet Union. This crucial fact has been obscured because Moscow and the West European CPs lack the nationalist antipathies that have so inflamed Sino-Soviet relations.

How, then, might such potentially divisive views as those postulated by the Italian and Spanish CPs become influential within the Soviet bloc? One way of approaching this question is to construct a spectrum of the political profiles to be found among the different European communist parties as a whole as well as, conceivably at least, within each individual CP. If this is done—from the Eurocommunists in the West to the remnants of Stalinism in the Soviet Union and East Europe—it may help to identify latent or actual transnational coalitions of like-minded groups or parties or both. To discern such coalitions is, in turn, of critical importance because they represent the channels of possible Eurocommunist influence within the socialist community.

For purposes of conceptual clarification, I shall designate four major categories on a scale from right to left: radical innovators, conservative innovators, conservative sectarians, and radical sectarians. The radical innovators are tantamount to the Eurocommunists, whose views have already been outlined. Let us begin, therefore, with the opposite end of the spectrum, the radical sectarians. On the fundamental issues of revolutionary strategy, socialist construction, and interparty relations, the radical sectarians generally tend to take the following positions. They urge communist control of every stage of the revolutionary process and deem both probable and acceptable the need for violence and manipulation on the path to power. Under socialism, they not only insist on a communist monopoly of power but also support the use of force, as needed, to achieve domestic goals. On questions of interparty affairs, they unabashedly uphold the leading role of the Soviet Union in the world communist movement as the cornerstone of proletarian internationalism. In short, their political mentality is neo-Stalinist. The current Czech regime as well as the Portuguese communists, especially if judged on the basis of their conduct in 1975, come closest to this rubric.

Immediately to the right of the radical sectarians are the conservative sectarians. They are at one with the radical sectarians on the need for communist control both during and after the revolution. They differ, however, in their preference for a peaceful, as opposed to a violent, march to power. Furthermore, they favor the use of incentives rather than force during the construction of socialism. Like the radical sectarians, they support Moscow's leading role in the communist movement. However, they advocate majority rule at world communist conferences as a means of legitimizing Soviet primacy. This category applies not so much to the parties of West Europe as to the party-states of East Europe in the post-Stalin era.

Next come the conservative innovators. Unlike the conservative sectarians' rather vague postulation of a peaceful revolution together with minority communist control, they specify the possibility of an electoral revolution along popular-front lines. In other words, they advocate a broad alliance strategy in which the communists command preponderant, but not total, authority and through which the Left may come to power by winning 51 percent of the vote. Under socialism, they envisage a continuation of communist preponderance but not necessarily exclusive CP control. Like the conservative sectarians, they prefer incentives to force. However, whereas the conservative sectarians link incentives to the co-optation of nonparty elites, the conservative innovators urge consultation with the nonparty groups in the policymaking process. As for interparty relations, they call for the operational rule of consensus, or veto power, in international communist forums—in contrast to the sectarians' support for Soviet primacy. Among the Western parties, the PCF most approximates the category of conservative innovators; the recurrent reform movements within the Soviet bloc party leaderships would also fall under this rubric.

As already noted, the radical innovators may be equated with the Eurocommunists, i.e., the PCI and the PCE. Briefly to recapitulate, their advocacy of a constitutional revolution amounts to support for liberal democracy prior to socialism. And under socialism, they anticipate that the working class as a whole, rather than its communist "vanguard" alone, will exercise hegemony. Their insistence on autonomy from Moscow leads them to favor interparty consultations on mutually relevant issues rather than formal conferences, whatever the operational rules. In the same vein, their support for cooperation among communists, socialists, and other political forces oriented toward socialism leads them to prefer the term *internationalist solidarity* to *proletarian internationalism.*

Having tentatively categorized the European CPs, the next question is whether the individual CPs can really be considered monolithic in outlook. In point of fact, all four categories may exist as latent group tendencies within most CPs. To classify a given party as belonging to only *one* category, therefore, is to distort reality by identifying the entire party with its dominant group or political center of gravity. To complicate matters further, the profile projected by a CP leadership may not be consistent with any of these categories. Owing to national peculiarities, it may embrace single facets of several points on our spectrum. Take the case of the Rumanians, who are conservative sectarians in domestic policy, conservative innovators in interparty relations, and radical innovators when speaking of revolution in the West. Or take the Yugoslavs, who are by and large conservative innovators on both domestic policy and interparty relations but sympathetic to the Eurocommunists on questions of revolutionary strategy. Then again, a leadership group may be divided—for example, on the question of revolutionary strategy or inter-CP relations—to the point where consistency is precluded.

The CPSU offers an example of a leadership group divided on a specific issue. The Soviet leaders are conservative sectarians in their postulation of "general laws" of socialist development and in their interpretation of proletarian internationalism. Yet on the nature of revolution in the West, they are of two minds, one rigidly sectarian and the other more innovative. A prominent exponent of the former view is Konstantin Zarodov, occasional *Pravda* commentator and editor in chief of *Problems of Peace and Socialism*—the Moscow-backed international communist political monthly based in Prague. In August 1975 Zarodov created a stir among Western CPs not only by stipulating communist hegemony as a precondition for revolutionary success but also by defining hegemony in terms of CP control of a "political" majority. He was in fact polemicizing against the conservative innovators' popular-front goal of a 51 percent victory. Zarodov subsequently rounded out his sectarian posture by denying the possibility of a purely constitutional left-wing victory and by calling violence inevitable in the revolutionary process.[2] By way of contrast, beginning in the winter of 1974-1975, a number of Soviet ideologues assumed a position on revolution in Europe that was essentially that of the conservative innovators. Men such as Boris Ponomarev, CPSU Secretariat member in charge of relations with nonruling CPs; Alekander Sobolev, editor in chief of *The Working Class and the Contemporary World* (a bimonthly Soviet journal founded in 1971 to deal with revolutionary trends); and Timur Timofeev, head of the Institute of the International Workers' Movement of the Soviet Academy of Sciences—all endorsed the popular-front strategy and, more generally, the need for a democratic transitional stage on the path to socialism in the West.[3] Vadim Zagladin, Ponomarev's deputy in charge of relations with West European CPs, reflected these more flexible views in his public utterances and, presumably, during backstage interparty negotiations.

Such internal party cleavages are significant not only in their own right but also because they offer opportunities for external involvement and influence. As a case in point, PCI spokesmen, most of whom are radical innovators in their political profile, have attacked Zarodov and praised Zagladin in their party press.[4] Similarly, when CPSU Politburo member Mikhail Suslov condemned Western CP regionalism as right opportunism in March 1976, a step that was extremely sectarian in its assumption of Soviet primacy, he was publicly rebuked by PCI Secretariat member Gianni Cervetti on the front page of *l'Unità*.[5] To be sure, the offending passage had been omitted from *Pravda*'s text of the Suslov speech—whether owing to opposition within the CPSU or also from Western communist sources remains unknown. Whatever the case, such public allusions to transnational group cleavages in the communist movement must be only the tip of the iceberg. At the same time, interparty group linkages need not be confined to official circles. The PCI, for instance, has also established ties with individuals deemed dissident by their own governments but who fall into the category of radical innovators. The Soviet historian Roy Medvedev is a well-known example. The PCI has carried accounts of Medvedev's unpublished *samizdat* writings in its daily paper, opened the pages of its more scholarly journals to his work, and even made private contact with him in Moscow.[6] Similarly, Italian Communist Central Committee member Lucio Lombardo Radice, more outspoken than most of his colleagues on the "inevitable" appeals of Eurocommunism in East Europe, publicly recounted in *l'Unità* his private talks with SED dissident Robert Havemann during the winter of 1977.[7]

In short, Eurocommunism views may penetrate the socialist community through transnational group linkages, whether of an official or unofficial character. However, the most effective channels of *influence*, i.e., of a policy impact, would appear to be contacts between radical or conservative innovators in the West and conservative officials in the East who are receptive to a more innovative line on specific issues.

Research Notes on the Impact of Eurocommunism

Circumstantial evidence indicates that the emergence of Eurocommunism did in fact influence certain political developments within the socialist community. On concrete issues there were shifts from a conservative sectarian policy to a more innovative policy, e.g., the official Soviet position on revolution in the West (Zarodov and company excepted). Moscow's stance on the June 1976 European CP summit also shifted. The Gierek regime in Poland seemed to back off its previous hard-line repression of domestic dissidents during the first half of 1977. During this same period Hungarian party chief János Kádár displayed public sympathy for the Eurocommunists, and the more sectarian leaders of Bulgaria and Czechoslovakia, doubtless with an eye on Moscow, mounted a campaign to discredit them as imperialist agents.

The secrecy of the decision making process among CP elites permits only educated guesses as to the extent or even presence of a Eurocommunist impact. Nevertheless, as will be discussed below, the coincidence in timing between Eurocommunist pressure or contacts, on the one hand, and the above-noted shifts, on the other, appears more than accidental. There is even less firm evidence about the channels through which the Eurocommunists may have influenced Soviet bloc elites. However, the antipathy between PCI spokesmen and conservative sectarians in the CPSU hierarchy suggests that the radical innovators would find receptive ears only among individuals of a more similar bent. They might be able to win over to their views a conservative innovator but not a sectarian of any ilk. At the same time, since the center of political gravity within the socialist community rests with the sectarians, a Eurocommunist linkage with would-be innovators in a Soviet bloc party would probably not in itself be sufficient to affect policy. The conservatives-turned-innovators would then have to use the Eurocommunist connection as leverage in their own internal party bargaining over policy options. The following discussion of concrete political shifts may flesh out these rather abstract suppositions.

Let us first look at the development of the CPSU's position on revolutionary strategy. From 1956 until the victory of

Allende's *Unidad Popular* coalition in the Chilean presidential elections of September 1970, Moscow endorsed the vague postulate of a peaceful parliamentary revolution in the West. As I have written elsewhere,[8] this in effect relegated revolution in the capitalist world to the indefinite future, as the Kremlin concentrated instead on achieving superpower parity and East-West deténte. Even during the West European ferment of the late 1960s, the CPSU, was preoccupied with securing control over Prague and ideological compliance from the communist movement as a whole, for example, at the June 1969 World Conference of Communist and Workers' Parties in Moscow. With Allende's accession to the Chilean presidency, however, such benign neglect of revolutionary prospects in the West was no longer feasible.

Moscow's theoretical posture on revolution in Chile turned out to be as sectarian as its practical response to the Dubček reform movement. In Chile as elsewhere, the communists were to play the leading role during the actual transition to socialism. In Soviet eyes the *Unidad Popular* government remained part of the "revolutionary-democratic" stage of historical development, and the characteristics of the more advanced socialist revolution were explicitly equated with those of the postwar East European people's democracies. It would appear that Moscow's stance on Chile was comparable to the Soviet reaction to developments in Czechoslovakia: namely, concessions to pluralism during the transition to socialism were as unacceptable as they were under socialism itself. Moreover, after Allende's overthrow in September 1973, CPSU ideologues verged on radical sectarianism as they demanded the destruction of the bourgeois state and the use of revolutionary illegality during any future revolutionary situation. The crushing of the *Unidad Popular* experiment by a military coup seemed to vindicate the Soviet proponents of revolutionary violence.

During late 1974 and early 1975, however, Moscow

abandoned not only its earlier neglect of revolutionary prospects in the West but also its more recent sectarian approach in favor of a policy of public support for the strategy of a democratic transitional stage.[9] This shift took the form of an elaboration of the CPSU's own long-standing call for a peaceful parliamentary revolution. The new approach was innovative in that it envisaged an electoral victory by majority vote. And it was gradualist in that it contemplated an intermediate stage between the overthrow of monopoly capitalism and the building of socialism. But it was also conservative in that it assumed that the communists would play the role of "vanguard" in the majoritarian revolution, that the CP would enjoy preponderant influence, if not total control, within a popular-front alliance.

Here it should be noted that all the major Western CPs were engrossed in what they saw as the most crucial issue: the formulation of an appropriate transitional strategy. They in fact supported quite different policies, depending on how they perceived their relative domestic strength and thus the imminence of their entry into an intermediate stage between capitalism and socialism. Among the Latin European parties, only the PCF hued closely to the Soviet interpretation of the democratic transitional stage. The Portuguese CP, for all its democratic professions during the fall and winter of 1974-1975, was actively infiltrating the Armed Forces Movement and trade unions with the apparent intent of bringing off a minority coup. In contrast, the PCI was spelling out its policy of a gradual pluralist revolution as "historic compromise" with Christian Democracy. The PCE was still groping for a way to bring down the Franco dictatorship. At first glance, nevertheless, all the Latin European CPs advocated some form of a transitional stage strategy.

It may be surmised, therefore, that Moscow viewed its endorsement of the strategy of a democratic transitional stage as an ideological vehicle to reassert its position as primus inter pares within the European communist movement. By acquiescing in the overall strategic orientation of the major West European CPs, it hoped to rally them to its side, at least on questions of interparty relations and eventual socialist construction. Specifically, the Kremlin leadership was bargaining for a public display of unity behind Moscow at the projected European CP summit as well as at a more distant world communist parley. At the same time, it doubtless reasoned that the strategy of a democratic transitional stage, insofar as it entailed activism without extremism, would not be unduly disruptive of East-West détente.

But why, it might be asked, did Moscow feel the need to bargain with the Western parties, to make concessions to them? Simply stated, in 1974 a revolutionary wave seemed to be on the rise in the West. The economic *cum* energy crisis, the Portuguese revolution, the French presidential race, the Italian divorce referendum, rumblings of discontent in Spain during the waning days of Franco's rule—the Latin European CPs were on the move, with or without Moscow's blessing. As for evidence that the CPSU was consciously making concessions at which it had hitherto balked, one need only look at Soviet-PCE relations. Since 1968 the Soviet sectarians and the Spanish radical innovators had been on the brink of schism, with Moscow supporting anti-Carrillo factions in the Spanish party. Yet in October 1974, on the eve of the first preparatory session for the East Berlin summit, the two parties signed a joint communique in which they agreed to disagree. The CPSU thereby gained the PCE's active participation in the preparations for the European CP conference. But the PCE came out ahead: it did not have to back down on its support for socialist pluralism and West European CP regionalism.[10] Not until 1977 did CPSU-PCE relations deteriorate to the status quo ante with the celebrated *New Times* attack on Carrillo's election pamphlet, *Eurocommunism and the State*.

Just as the strategy of the democratic transitional stage became the dominant Soviet posture on revolution in the West after 1974, so too Moscow's approach to interparty relations was modified, or at least circumscribed, during the twenty months of negotiations leading to the East Berlin summit. Here there is considerable evidence that the CPSU made concessions to the Eurocommunists and their allies (the PCF, the Yugoslavs, the Rumanians).[11] First of all, agreement by consensus rather than majority rule (because of the pro-Soviet posture of most smaller CPs, a code word for CPSU predominance) became the procedural principle of the Berlin conference. This was in marked contrast to the 1960 world CP conference, where Khrushchev's insistence on the majority principle drove the Chinese into open opposition, or the 1969 rump world CP conference, where a similar attitude on the part of the Brezhnev leadership led the Rumanian and Spanish CPs to append reservations to the final resolution, the Italians to abstain on major portions of the resolution, and the Yugoslavs to boycott the conference altogether (as they had done in 1960).[12] Second, given the consensus rule, any mention at Berlin of "general laws" of socialist construction was precluded, and only the broadest conception of socialist revolution was possible. In the end Moscow pushed neither issue; and the final document of the Berlin meeting was silent on the characteristics of socialism and open-ended on the nature of revolution, referring only to "respect for the free choice of different paths . . . to socialism."[13]

The critical issue during the last six months or so of pre-conference bargaining, therefore, became the norms of interparty relations to be observed by members of the European communist movement. The Soviet press not only insisted on the principle of "proletarian internationalism"; it also included under this principle the rejection of any criticism of Soviet reality, equating all such criticism with anticommunism.[14] Moscow seemed receptive to the inclusion of communist-socialist cooperation under the rubric of proletarian internationalism. Yet since few socialists could be expected to forgo their right to criticize the Soviet Union, the CPSU leaders were simply giving with one hand what they took away with the other. Ultimately, however, they had to back down even on this point in order to reach a consensus. The conference document thus rejected the very term *proletarian internationalism* in favor of internationalist solidarity. It also specified that "Communists don't consider as anti-Communists all those . . . who express a critical attitude toward their activity," thereby legitimizing anti-Soviet criticism. Most significantly, perhaps, the Berlin document set forth a standard by which to exercise that right of criticism by pledging to uphold the Helsinki principles of respect for "the rights of man and fundamental liberties, including freedom of thought, conscience, religion or creed."

That the CPSU agreed only reluctantly to the Berlin document was clear from its continued use of the term *proletarian internationalism* and from its denunciation of anti-Soviet criticism. Despite occasional references to "internationalism and contemporary development" attended by publicists from the Warsaw Pact nations (Rumania excepted), Vadim Zagladin spelled out the need to retain the term even while broadening its content to include sociopolitical forces of diverse ideological inspiration.[15] At the same time, the *New Times* attack on Carrillo in June 1977 left no doubts about the CPSU's intolerance of anti-Soviet criticism.

Why did the Soviet leadership acquiesce in East Berlin to formulations so contrary to its own preferences? One must look first to the consensus principle and then to the cleavages that developed within the European communist movement during the preparations for the summit. From the outset of the preparatory talks in late 1974, the consensus rule allowed for the possibility that one or another party might boycott the summit because its views were not respected. In the early stages only the Spanish and Yugoslav parties appeared likely candidates for such a role. But the sudden rift between the French and Soviet parties in the autumn of 1975 tipped the scales in favor of the CP innovators. The PCF, for reasons probably related to domestic political calculations, began criticizing Soviet repression of dissidents and passivity toward revolution as Moscow geared up for the Twenty-Fifth CPSU Congress (which George Marchais boycotted). The French shift to the side of the Eurocommunists (the PCI and PCE) and the East European mavericks on interparty ties (Yugoslavia and Rumania) made both groups more respectable. The Yugoslavs and Rumanians were no longer tainted by exclusive reliance on the radical innovators in their opposition to Soviet-style proletarian internationalism. By the same token, the Spanish and Italian parties found in their new regional entente with the PCF (highlighted by the PCI-PCF and PCE-PCF joint communiques of November 1975) a claim to legitimacy and counterweight to Portuguese communist sectarianism. The nonconformist coalition had grown to the point where its refusal to go along with the pro-Soviet majority could no longer be passed off as revisionist obstructionism. If the negotiations for the Berlin conference had collapsed, communists and noncommunists alike would have blamed it on Soviet domineering. In effect, the burden of giving in or copping out had suddenly shifted to Moscow. The CPSU therefore gave in at East Berlin only to try and cover up the fact, at least within the socialist community, through distorted media coverage of what actually happened at the summit. Yet Soviet distortion notwithstanding, the Berlin document remained a reference point for CP conduct in East Europe as well as in West Europe.

After the Berlin conference, a number of political trends in East Europe also seemed to be shaped by the growing visibility of the Eurocommunists. In the "northern tier" of the GDR, Poland, and Czechoslovakia, on the one hand, there was an upsurge in dissident activity by individuals often publicly aligned with the radical innovators in the West. Jacek Kuron[16] and Edward Lipiński[17] of the Polish Workers' Defense Committee and Zdenek Mlynar[18] of the Czech "Charter 77" group, among others, publicly praised the Western CP reformers or appealed to them for support against sectarian policies at home. This increase in dissident activity provoked, in turn, a sectarian backlash in Czechoslovakia and Bulgaria (less so in the GDR) against both the dissidents and their Eurocommunist allies. In the December 1976 issue of Konstantin Zarodov's journal, Bulgarian party leader Todor Zhivkov hailed solidarity with the Soviet Union as the "touchstone" of proletarian internationalism—a phrase harking back to the Comintern days. He then declared Eurocommunism to be a bourgeois tool designed to split and subvert the international communist movement.[19] And immediately after the publication of "Charter 77" in January 1977, the Czechoslovak party media started accusing its supporters of being agents of "anti-Communist and Zionist centers."

On the other hand, the Polish and Hungarian party chiefs' approach to dissent and Eurocommunism was rather innovative, especially when compared to their neighbors' sectarian rigidity. János Kádár expressed confidence in the Eurocommunists at press conferences held in Austria in December 1976 and Italy and West Germany in June 1977.[20] The occasions were in themselves notable in that Kádár had rarely visited the West since the Hungarian revolution of 1956. As for domestic dissent, some three dozen or so Hungarian cultural figures signed a letter of solidarity with the "Charter 77" group without eliciting any official reaction.[21] It would appear that the self-assurance and clout of the Kádár regime, since 1968 the flag-bearer of conservative innovation in the Soviet bloc, had been enhanced by the emergence of a grouping clearly to its right within the

European communist movement. About this same time Polish party leader Edward Gierek began speaking of the need for political struggle rather than police action in dealing with the ongoing ferment sparked by the June 1976 price riots in the outskirts of Warsaw.

Since mid-1976 there had been more and more indications of a division within the Polish party leadership between sectarians and innovators, between those urging greater administrative and police control and those favoring more incentives and popular consultation.[22] The arbitrary increases in food prices and their equally abrupt cancellation in response to the workers' demonstrations were perhaps the most visible signs of this cleavage. But equally telling was the regime's subsequent vacillation as unrest spread from workers to cultural figures, students, and even church spokesmen. The arrest and rough treatment of hundreds of workers after the June 1976 riots was superseded by a broad amnesty in February 1977. Meanwhile the members of the small but militant Workers' Defense Committee suffered harassment but not incarceration. Then, in May 1977, after student demonstrations in Kraków protesting the mysterious death of a youthful dissident, several members of the Workers' Defense Committee were arrested—only to be pardoned and released on July 22 (Poland's National Day), 1977, along with the remaining workers imprisoned in June 1976. On balance, therefore, the Polish regime seemed to tilt toward conservative innovation.

Indeed, Edward Gierek's public statements during the spring of 1977 marked him as an innovator in the East European context. At the April plenum of the Central Committee, he advocated the use against dissent of "political methods and arguments"—code words in the communist lexicon for persuasion rather than repression. Several months later he urged tolerance toward religious opponents, this after an unprecedented involvement of churchmen in the May protest movement. Moreover, at the April plenum

Gierek proclaimed the strengthening of "socialist democracy" as the order of the day. This could be viewed as unexceptional rhetoric were it not for the appearance about the same time of an article in the party's theoretical journal, *Nowe Drogi,* suggesting an electoral reform permitting some degree of genuine choice to the Polish people.[23] Gierek's more innovative stance on domestic issues had its counterpart in his approach to interparty affairs. Not only did the Polish party cosponsor (with the PCI) the Berlin conference of European CPs, but in mid-June 1976 Gierek also expressed sympathetic understanding for the PCI's support of Italy's continued membership in NATO.[24]

But how did the Italian Communist leadership react to the Polish situation? As the largest contingent among the radical innovators, the PCI and its relationship with the Polish party are critical to any assessment of Eurocommunist influence on the socialist community.

Two distinct patterns emerged in the PCI media's coverage of the Polish ferment of 1976-1977. First of all, *l'Unità* took an evenhanded posture toward the regime and dissidents alike. The same article would often present both the official line and the opposition's interpretation of a given incident. For example, it cited both the government denials of police brutality toward workers arrested in June 1976 and statements to the contrary by the Workers' Defense Committee. *L'Unità* gave similar treatment to the popular protests over the untoward death of the Kraków youth in May 1977. What is significant here is that it refrained from any editorial criticism of the Polish party's conduct. Only a close reading of the ostensibly straight news reports reveals that the Italian party actually sympathized with the dissidents. This approach contrasted sharply with the PCI's coverage of dissent and repression in Czechoslovakia and the Soviet Union during the same period. In both these cases, *l'Unità* first juxtaposed the official line to the dissidents' views, for instance, with regard to "Charter 77" or the Soviet human rights activists; it then proceeded to lambast editorially the conduct of the Czech and Soviet regimes.[25]

The second distinctive aspect of the PCI's relation to Polish developments was its cautiously constructive commentaries in the party's political weekly, *Rinascita*. In effect, the Italian communists assumed the mantle of conservative innovators in their policy recommendations for the Polish regime. A major *Rinascita* piece in December 1976 linked the resolution of Poland's political and economic problems to more consultation between decision makers and the major Polish social groups: the workers, intellectuals, and largely Catholic peasants. It specified, moreover, that the peasants should be organized through their natural representative, the church. In short, the PCI did not call for Western-style political pluralism. It did not question the Polish party's leading role, merely the way in which it exercised that role.[26]

The reasons for the PCI's relative restraint are not difficult to fathom. Given the apparent cleavage between sectarians and innovators within the Polish leadership, the Italian party doubtless sought to bring its prestige to bear on the side of the innovators. To this end it refrained from outright criticism of the Warsaw regime, perhaps fearing that public censure might put the innovators on the defensive or even tilt the scales against them in the internal party jousting for the upper hand. For the same reason PCI spokesmen suggested policies that were presumably favored by the Polish reformers. More direct PCI involvement in the inner struggles of the Polish party is a subject of conjecture at best. However, several bits of information lend themselves to speculation in this regard. For example, when Gierek announced a partial amnesty on February 3, 1977, Antonio Rubbi, deputy head of the PCI Central Committee's International Section and public polemicist against such Soviet sectarians as Zarodov, was in Warsaw on an official party visit. Was Rubbi's presence coincidental? Or was it a sign that the PCI's policy of cautious encouragement to the

The Impact of Eurocommunism

Polish innovators was bearing fruit? Then on July 2, 1977, *l'Unità* praised Gierek for favoring tolerance and dialogue to frontal clashes with dissidents.[27] At that very same time a top-level PCI delegation was in Moscow protesting the Soviet leadership's frontal clash with Santiago Carrillo in *New Times,* the authorities in Warsaw had apparently not been decided whether to release the Workers' Defense Committee members arrested in May. Was *l'Unità*'s praise of Gierek an attempt to strengthen the hand of the Polish moderates during the negotiations leading to the July amnesty? Was it part of the PCI's larger détente with the CPSU over the norms of conduct to be observed among communists? Or was it a bit of both? The answer will probably never be known.

The preceding discussion has brought to light largely circumstantial evidence of a Eurocommunist impact on the socialist community. Nevertheless, the cumulative weight of the available clues lends support to the hypothesis suggested earlier in this chapter: the very existence of the Eurocommunists gives more leeway to the more reform-minded elites within the Soviet bloc parties. No longer relegated to the "right wing" of the officially tolerated political spectrum, these East European reformers are able to use Eurocommunist support as leverage against their more sectarian comrades. Specifically, on questions pertaining to the European communist movement as a whole, they are able to exercise leverage through the formation of informal coalitions with Western CPs. This was the case during the preparations for the Berlin conference. As became clear during the shaping of the final conference document, the application of the consensus rule to the summit proceedings led to bargaining and compromise among shifting coalitions of ruling and nonruling CPs. Moreover, the document itself further enhanced the maneuverability of the Soviet bloc innovators by giving formal sanction to CP diversity and mutual criticism—not to mention nonalignment as practiced by Yugoslavia.

Furthermore, transnational coalitions of like-minded CP groupings also seem on occasion to play a role in the resolution of internal-party differences in the socialist community. Here, of course, the possibility for Eurocommunist involvement hinges upon the presence of a fairly influential reform faction in one or another ruling party. That, in turn, is contingent upon a host of particular domestic circumstances, such as those that differentiate Poland and Hungary from Bulgaria and Czechoslovakia.

As for the intentions of the Eurocommunists, they probably prefer to bolster the forces of conservative rather than radical innovation in the domestic policies of the socialist community. If history is any guide to the future, political pluralism as understood in the West has little prospect of success within the Soviet bloc. This is not to say that the Eurocommunists feel no kinship with their radical counterparts in the East. Their defense of dissent and denunciation of repression in Eastern Europe bespeak their sentiments. Yet reason dictates caution. As indicated by the PCI's approach to Polish developments, the Eurocommunists seem well aware that to foster *radical* innovation would play into the hands of the sectarians and to invite repression of *all* innovative tendencies. Besides, the Western CP reformers surely understand that if the dominant influence in a ruling party shifts from conservative sectarianism to conservative innovation, there would be, if not a systemic change, at least a substantial improvement in the quality of life for the population involved. Indeed, the consumerism and decentralized decision making advocated by the conservative innovators may well be as significant in the long run as the remission of terror wrought by the conservative sectarians a generation ago: thus, the Eurocommunists may be expected to do their utmost to avoid a rupture with Moscow, which could spell the end of their moderating influence in Soviet bloc affairs.

Notes

1. For a comparison of PCF and PCI criticism of Soviet bloc systems during the autumn of 1976 and the winter of 1977, see my "West European Communist Parties and the Soviet Union" (Paper written for the U.S. Department of State Conference on the Foreign Policy of Eurocommunism, May 12-14, 1977).

2. See, for example, Zarodov's commentaries in *Pravda*, August 6, 1975, and August 26, 1977.

3. The development of this position is treated in my "Contemporary Soviet Perspectives on Revolution in the West," *Orbis* 19, no. 4 (Winter 1976): 1359-1402.

4. For example, Adriano Guerra, "Su democrazia e socialismo," *l'Unità*, February 19, 1976, p. 3; and Antonio Rubbi, "Berlino, oltre le polemiche," *Rinascita*, July 30, 1976, pp. 9-10.

5. "I communisti italiani e l'internazionalismo: A proposito di un articolo del compagno Suslov," *l'Unità*, March 28, 1976, pp. 1, 21.

6. For example, "Uno scritto dello storico Medvedev sui problemi del socialismo," *l'Unità*, March 17, 1976, p. 13; and Roy A. Medvedev, "La rivoluzione d'Ottobre fu prematura?" *Studi storici* 17, no. 2 (1976): 5-26; cf. Christopher S. Wren, "Italian Reds in Visit to Soviet Dissident," *New York Times,* January 30, 1977, p. 7.

7. "Incontro con Havemann," *l'Unità*, March 2, 1977, p. 3.

8. Urban, "Contemporary Soviet Perspectives on Revolution in the West," pp. 1359-1365.

9. Ibid.

10. Eusebio M. Mujal-Leon, "Spanish Communism in the 1970's," *Problems of Communism* 24, no. 2 (March-April 1975): 43-55.

11. For a masterful account of the preparations for the Berlin summit, see Kevin Devlin, "The Challenge of Eurocommunism," *Problems of Communism* 26, no. 1 (January-February 1977); 1-20.

12. Cf. Kevin Devlin, "The Interparty Drama," *Problems of Communism* 24, no. 4 (July-August 1975): 18-34. In 1968, the Chinese, Albanian, North Vietnamese, and North Korean CPs, as well as several small, sectarian, nonruling parties, did not officially participate.

13. The full text was published in the Soviet weekly, *New Times,* July 28, 1976, pp. 17-32.

14. For authoritative statements to this effect, see Vitalii

Korionov, "Znamia kommunistov," *Pravda,* January 24, 1976, p. 4; and Vadim Zagladin, "Internatsionalizm—Znamia kommunistov," ibid., April 20, 1976, pp. 3-4.

15. Reported in *l'Unità,* March 10, 1977, p. 14.

16. "Lettera aperta d'un 'dissidente' polacco a Berlinguer," ibid., July 20, 1976, p. 14.

17. "An Open Letter to Comrade Edward Gierek," text in *Survey* 22, no. 2 (Spring 1976): 194-203.

18. Mlynar's appeal to West European CPs and socialists for intervention in behalf of arrested "Charter 77" signatories was reported in *l'Unità,* January 19 and 20, 1977, pp. 12 and 10, respectively.

19. "Year of peace, year of struggle," *World Marxist Review* 19, no. 12 (December 1976): 3-15.

20. Reported in the *New York Times,* December 8, 1976; and *l'Unità,* June 10 and July 1, 1977.

21. See "Adesioni alla lettera aperta di intellettuali ungheresi," *l'Unità,* January 22, 1977, p. 14; cf. ibid., January 21, 1977, p. 11.

22. For a penetrating analysis, see the two-part feature by Manuel Lucbert, "La Pologne entre le miel et le vinaigre," *Le Monde,* July 23, 1977, pp. 1 and 4, and July 24-25, 1977, p. 4.

23. Ibid.

24. Gierek interview with *Der Spiegel* reported in *l'Unità,* July 17, 1976, p. 15.

25. See my "West European Communist Parties and the Soviet Union."

26. Franco Bertrone, "Polonia: le radici della tensione," *Rinascita,* December 10, 1976, pp. 21-22.

27. Silvio Trevisani, "Come la Polonia affronta la difficile congiuntura," *l'Unità,* July 2, 1977, p. 14.

Part 3
The International Environment as Innovator

8. U.S. Foreign Policy as Agent of Change in Communism

Robert S. Wood

President Jimmy Carter assumed the presidency with an inaugural statement clearly weighted toward national modesty and away from grand designs, even rhetorical ones: "We have learned that 'more' is not necessarily 'better,' that even our great nation has its recognized limits and that we can neither answer all questions nor solve all problems. We cannot afford to do everything."[1] Indeed, in a real sense, the Carter administration seemed to be reacting not only against the "overextension" of the 1960s and early 1970s generally, but also specifically against the globalism of Henry Kissinger. Both the summons of John F. Kennedy—"we shall pay any price, bear any burden, meet any hardship... to assure the survival and the success of liberty"—and Kissinger's design for a linked structure of peace appeared to be suspect.

Within a matter of days after the inaugural, however, the president seemed to be stating a conception of foreign policy aimed not simply at influencing the international behavior of states but at modifying the basic character of their regimes. That such a policy was not merely limited to self-contained rhetoric or domestic effects is seen by such diverse, yet related, initiatives as the issuance of a State Department report on human rights in Brazil and a subsequent report on eighty-one other countries; the suspension or reduction of military assistance to Ethiopia, Argentina, and Uruguay; the reception of Soviet dissidents in the White House; and the recommendation for congressional support for eleven new transmitters for Radio Liberty/Radio Free Europe. A host of such moves affected relations with communist and noncommunist countries around the globe and apparently had some influence on such ongoing negotiations as the strategic arms limitation talks.

There has been a recent moderation in the Carter human rights campaign, as evidenced in the administration's opposition to attempted congressional requirements that U.S. representatives to international lending agencies automatically vote against credits for governments violating human rights. Nonetheless, one can be excused for wondering whether the Carter administration's conception of foreign policy is more extended and less modest than any in recent times. This suspicion is kindled not only by human rights campaigns but also by extraordinary assertions that one of the president's objectives is the total elimination of nuclear weapons. At the same time, however, the administration's reluctance to provide open or clandestine military support to friendly Third World states under attack, the manifest desire to withdraw troops from South Korea, and the growing ambiguity as to the proper use of economic tools—all may point to a situation in which moralism will cover, consciously or unconsciously, a policy of withdrawal, self-reliance, and isolation across the whole spectrum of concerns from energy to military security. More probably, the sometimes contradictory evidence simply indicates that the Carter policy is still inchoate, characterized more by impulses than design, grand or otherwise.

In any case, the Carter administration has revived the question of U.S. foreign policy as an agent of change in communism and has asserted conceptual principles diametrically opposed to those that animated the stewardship of Henry Kissinger.

Intervention against Communism

Western initiatives to modify or overthrow communist regimes are as old as the Bolshevik revolution itself. In December 1917, the British and French governments entered into agreements aimed at the clandestine finance and support of anti-Bolshevik factions in southern Russia, and, of course, there were direct Western interventions in northern Russia and Siberia. To a large degree, however, these involvements were prompted less by ideological animus than by concern for the progress of the war against Germany. As George F. Kennan remarked of the north Russian engagement: "The decisions were military decisions, taken in strict wartime secrecy. . . . The simple fact remains: had a world war not been in progress, there would never, under any conceivable stretch of the imagination, have been an Allied intervention in North Russia."[2]

Of course, Western analysis has generally assumed that Soviet external behavior is animated to some substantial degree by the hostile visions of its totalitarian-communist ideology, if only by an ideologically induced exaggeration of its security concerns. From this perspective, the character of the Soviet regime is hence by no means irrelevant to the foreign policy concerns of the United States.

George Kennan, in the Mr. X *Foreign Affairs* article of 1947, stated that "the maintenance of this pattern of Soviet power, namely, the pursuit of unlimited authority domestically, accompanied by the cultivation of the semi-myth of implacable foreign hostility, has gone far to shape the actual machinery of Soviet power as we know it today."[3] A historically authoritarian culture and polity in Russia was joined with an ideology totalitarian in its intellectual structure to produce a regime whose reach might know no limits, whatever conservatism it may demonstrate within the limits of its capabilities and a given geopolitical environment. Moreover, given the confidence of the regime in historical inevitability and in its own infallible understanding thereof, the Soviet government was seen as governed by a sense of patience and control. Hence, Kennan argued, "it will be clearly seen that the Soviet pressure against the free institutions of the western world is something that can be contained by the adroit and vigilant application of counter-force at a series of constantly shifting geographical and political points, corresponding to the shift and maneuvers of Soviet policy, but which cannot be charmed or talked out of existence. The Russians look forward to a duel of infinite duration."[4] Thus were enunciated the doctrine of containment and the notion of protracted conflict.

Containment was not to be conceived simply as a counterbalancing of the external thrusts of Soviet power, but as a potential modifier of the character of the Soviet regime itself. As Kennan observed:

> The future of Soviet power may not be by any means as secure as Russian capacity for self-delusion would make it appear to the men in the Kremlin. . . . But the possibility remains (and in the opinion of this writer it is a strong one) that Soviet power, like the capitalist world of its conception, bears within it the seeds of its own decay, and that the sprouting of these seeds is well advanced.
> It is clear that the United States cannot expect in the foreseeable future to enjoy political intimacy with the Soviet regime. It must continue to regard the Soviet Union as a rival, not a partner, in the political arena. It must continue to expect that Soviet policies will reflect no abstract love of peace and stability, no real faith in the possibility of a permanent happy coexistence of the Socialist and capitalist worlds, but rather a cautious, persistent pressure toward the disruption and weakening of all rival influence and rival power.
> Balanced against this are the facts that Russia, as opposed to the western world in general, is still by far the weaker

party, that Soviet policy is highly flexible, and that Soviet society may well contain deficiencies which will eventually weaken its own total potential. This would of itself warrant the United States entering with reasonable confidence upon a policy of firm containment, designed to confront the Russians with unalterable counter-force at every point where they show signs of encroaching upon the interests of a peaceful and stable world.

But in actuality the possibilities for American policy are by no means limited to holding the line and hoping for the best. It is entirely possible for the United States to influence by its actions the internal developments, both within Russia and throughout the international Communist movement, by which Russian policy is largely determined. This is not only a question of the modest measure of informational activity which this government can conduct in the Soviet Union and elsewhere, although that, too, is important. It is rather a question of the degree to which the United States can create among the peoples of the world generally the impression of a country which knows what it wants, which is coping successfully with the problems of its internal life and with the responsibilities of a World Power, and which has a spiritual validity capable of holding its own among the major ideological currents of the time. To the extent that such an impression can be created and maintained, the aims of Russian Communism must appear sterile and quixotic, the hopes and enthusiasm of Moscow's supporters must wane, and added strain must be imposed on the Kremlin's foreign policies. For the palsied decrepitude of the capitalist world is the keystone of Communist philosophy. Even the failure of the United States to experience the early economic depression which the ravens of the Red Square have been predicting with such complacent confidence since hostilities ceased would have deep and important repercussions throughout the Communist world.[5]

Even without Kennan's later glosses on this article, it is clear that his recommendations were not aimed at an adventuristic policy of liberation. It is equally clear that internally generated and externally assisted modifications in the character of the communist regime were critical elements in the notion of containment. It is precisely these latter assumptions that disturbed a contemporary commentator such as Walter Lippman and latter-day converts such as J. William Fulbright. Lippman argued shortly after the publication of the article: "My objection then to the policy of containment is not that it seeks to confront the Soviet power with American power, but that the policy is misconceived, and must result in a misuse of American power.... It commits the country to a struggle which has for its objective nothing more substantive than the hope that in ten or fifteen years the Soviet power will, as a result of long frustration, 'break up' or 'mellow'."[6] In Lippman's view, such a policy in the first instance conceded the strategic initiative to the Soviet Union and provided the United States no fair gauge of its genuine international interests, and in the second instance, it would lead us to consider too seriously ideological, as opposed to more modest geostrategic, questions: "It was the mighty power of the Red Army, not the ideology of Karl Marx, which enabled the Russian government to expand its frontiers."[7] In this view, U.S. policy must hence come to terms with the persistence of the geopolitical entity of Russia. Through political maneuvers, military alliances, and bargaining with the Soviet Union, a balance of power must be constructed that would inhibit the external thrust of Soviet power. In 1947 Lippman saw this as best expressed in the problem of "how the continent of Europe can be evacuated by the three non-European armies which are now inside Europe."[8] In his view, therefore,

> the withdrawal of the army is, therefore, the acid test of Soviet conduct and purpose, incomparably clearer, more definite, more practical than whether or not they observe the Yalta Declaration in countries liberated from the Nazis but still occupied by the Red Army. Verbal agreements like the Yalta Declaration and the Atlantic Charter can be made the subject of endless tactical maneuvering. For agreements of this kind do not change the balance of power. But the evacuation of a continent would change the balance of power.... It is to the Red Army in Europe, therefore, and not to ideologies,

elections, forms of government, to socialism, to communism, to free enterprise, that a correctly conceived and soundly planned policy should be directed.[9]

One may justifiably argue that in practical terms a policy more attentive to ideology versus one more concerned with direct external effects was not that starkly drawn in the general policy of the United States in the postwar period. Nonetheless, there are at play here two general tendencies that, depending on one's emphases, could give a different texture and rationalization of policy.

Carter and Human Rights

Speaking before the United Nations, President Carter enunciated the basis for the U.S. campaign for human rights: "The basic thrust of human affairs points toward a more universal demand for fundamental human rights. The United States has a historical birthright to be associated with this process."[10] Carter's reference to the American birthright points both to the character of the U.S. regime and to the faith that is most critical to an understanding of Carter's approach to foreign policy—that is, his faith in the civil religion. Certain important assumptions undergird discussions of U.S. policy—whether internal or external. They constitute the moral justification of policy initiatives and the bedrock of American legitimacy. In brief, these assumptions include:

1. the primacy of the individual endowed with rights natural rather than exclusively civil in character. Groups of course have status, but their legitimacy derives from the individual rights and interests they express. Hence, loyalty to the group is decisively qualified by individual interests or by transcendental individual rights. The contingent nature of loyalty and obedience is as true of the state as it is of any other group;

2. the consequent necessity of the consent of the governed in the organization of any social group, including the state;
3. the right of rebellion against a regime that systematically denies these rights or ignores consent logically follows from the notion of natural individual rights and the principle of consent;
4. the belief that since fundamental rights are natural rather than civil in origin, all mankind shares in these rights and constitutes a universal community prior to and ultimately transcending any historical state;
5. the duty, therefore, of the American Republic is both to enunciate these universal principles and to favor their realization whenever possible. As John Winthrop stated as early as 1630, "The eyes of all people are upon us . . . we shall be made a story and a byword through the world . . . we shall be a city upon a hill";[11]
6. the conviction that the safety of the nation depends ultimately not on the protection of distance, terrain, or weapons, but fidelity to the founding principles of the republic. As Lincoln expressed it:

> Shall we expect some trans-Atlantic military giant to step the ocean and crush us at a blow? Never—all the armies of Europe, Asia and Africa combined, with all the treasure of the earth in their military chest, with a Bonaparte for a commander, could not by force take a drink from the Ohio or make a track on the Blue Ridge in a trial of a thousand years. At what point then is the approach of danger to be expected? I answer, if it ever reaches us, it must spring up amongst us—it cannot come from abroad. If destruction be our lot, we must ourselves be its author and finisher. As a nation of free men, we must live through all time, or die by suicide.[12]

It was to this faith that Carter summoned the nation in his inaugural—"the bold and brilliant dream which excited the founders of our nation still awaits its consummation. I have no new dream to set forth today, but rather urge a fresh faith in the old dream."[13]

It is thus likely that President Carter was quite genuine in his February 23, 1977, news conference when he remarked:

> So I think we all ought to take a position in our own country and among our friends and allies, among our potential adversaries, that human rights is something on which we should bear a major responsibility for leadership, and I have made it clear to the Soviet Union and to others in the Eastern Europe Community that I'm not trying to launch a unilateral criticism of them, that I'm trying to set a standard in our own country and make my concerns expressed throughout the world, not singled out against any particular country.[14]

But it is equally true that the president's principles of human rights are at their core fundamentally antithetical to the very foundation of the Marxist regimes. It seems likely, therefore, that major emphasis on human rights could overshadow any point of convergence between American and Soviet interests. There may be more than humor in the recent exchange in "Doonesbury" between an eager freshman and the unseen visiting professor, Dr. Henry Kissinger, in which the good doctor patiently noted that a human rights campaign could not but be subversive of the Soviet regime.

If the basic assumptions of the American polity can be briefly noted, so too can the principles and perspectives of the Soviet and East European regimes:

1. The primacy of the group is asserted, and the freedom of the individual consists in his proper relationship to that collectivity, which gives his life meaning and direction.
2. History constitutes a dialectical struggle among groups whose status and character are determined by their relationship to the means of production.
3. As the goal of history is the elimination of alienation and all forms of exploitation, the proletariat repre-

sents the favored object of history and the party the ordained instrument.
4. The characteristic feature of history is thus conflict, and the only unity of mankind is biological, not moral.
5. A community of mankind can emerge only at the end of history, and thus universal notions of right apart from the specific position of one's group in the class struggle are formalistic and reactionary.
6. Government authority is legitimately exercised only by the collective that is true to the authentic revolutionary direction of history.

Within the context of this thought, *Pravda*'s explanation of the "Brezhnev doctrine" is completely intelligible: "Law and legal norms are subjected to the laws of the class struggle, the laws of social development."[15]

The Soviets are fully cognizant of the radical distinction between Marxist and liberal thought—and indeed have based their notion of peaceful coexistence upon this disjuncture. They have consistently insisted that "the sphere of class and national-liberation struggle" cannot be brought within "peaceful coexistence" and that, indeed, détente has given "a powerful impulse to the national-liberation movement of colonial and oppressed people." Brezhnev has argued that détente is a result of "a new relationship of forces"—that is, the ascendancy of the Soviet-socialist forces. Hence, as an *Izvestiia* commentator recently contended, "the process of détente does not mean and never meant the freezing of the social-political status quo in the world," and in fact nothing could or should prevent the Soviet Union from giving "sympathy, compassion, and support" to these forces of "national liberation." In my view, then, détente or peaceful coexistence involves direct state relations between the United States and the Soviet Union, particularly in the strategic area, but is not designed to prevent Soviet support for "favorable developments" in various third states.[16]

Precisely because of the Soviet notion of coexistence, many have applauded Carter's elevation of the ideological banner. It is felt that such a policy reintroduces a degree of symmetry in our relations. The human rights campaign legitimizes our concern with non-Western, Third World states and our apprehensions about Soviet penetration; it provides a continued avenue of access to the populations of Eastern Europe and perhaps even to the subject nationalities of the Soviet Union; it allows us to raise, if at times obliquely, questions concerning the real dedication to liberal democracy of the Western communist parties, still wedded to the Marxian world view. And to the degree that Carter believes in the unnaturalness of the Soviet leadership as men in the "natural light of reason," the human rights campaign provides not simply an instrument in the strategy of conflict but the basis of a genuine rational dialogue. Moreover, there is the hope that the convergence of our interests in such areas as strategic weapons is so solid that one can indeed detach the human rights campaign from various interstate relations. There is no doubt that there is important symmetry between this line of reasoning and Brezhnev's peaceful coexistence. There is also no doubt that the previous administration rejected this logic as counterproductive and dangerous.

Westphalian Principles and the Diplomacy of Henry Kissinger

In the century after the Treaty of Westphalia (1648), the European state system was established on the political principle of territoriality and on the legal principle of sovereign equality. The former entailed the effective control by the major princes within established territorial limits, and the second established the norm of complete political jurisdiction by the prince and his government within these territorial boundaries, jurisdiction unencumbered by any earthly, external authority. Although states were unequal in material capabilities and political influence, they confronted one another in the international arena under the obligation to recognize one another as masters within their territorial domains. And, in the intercourse of states, agreements were to be based on the norm of contracts, explicit or implicit, among equal partners, whatever the actual political realities underlying their calculus. States organized not by a supranational power but by the sovereign agreement of these states—this was to be the pattern of modern nonintervention and domestic jurisdiction—princes may meet one another in battle and adjust the political map of Europe, but they must resist the urge to influence too blatantly—by direct or covert intervention—the character of one another's type of regime and ideological commitment. That this conception of international affairs was realized only imperfectly is obvious, but that it provided an influential normative frame of action is also clear.

The evolution of the principles of the modern state system is attributable in the first instance to the experiences of the emergent states from the fourteenth to the sixteenth centuries. Various princes were trying to separate their domain from an empire, the Catholic church had supranational pretensions, and finally, the Reformation divided Christendom; as a result, the politics of the period were suffused with a harsh ideological cast, and political regimes and territorial boundaries were problematical. The culmination was the Thirty Years' War. The partial stalemate among the states and the jeopardy in which intervention placed every regime persuaded Europe's political leadership to evolve a system that would better guarantee the stability of the states. The key was to separate international relations from internal politics. The separation was never complete, and the smaller states were never as certainly covered by the new norms as the great states, but international relations in rough-and-ready fashion did conform to the new pattern until the wars of the French Revolution and Napoleon.

With the French Revolution, the character of regimes

again became a stake in the international conflict, and ideological concerns again interacted with power political motives. The defeat of Napoleon largely restored prerevolutionary notions, which, despite the strains of nationalism, class ideologies, and racial doctrines, persisted until World War I. Since that great war, however, the world has been buffeted by supranational ideologies and ambitions cloaked in universal principles whose very intensity erodes political boundaries and casts doubt on the distinction between domestic and international politics. Moreover, with the rise of a multitude of weak and divided states unable to establish domestic order and resist foreign incursions, the problem of distinguishing levels of political activity and limiting political ambitions is exacerbated. Some observers have further cited the interdependence of the international economy as another force in the erosion of the classical principles of the modern state system. In such a "revolutionary" situation, then, what is the role of the doctrine of nonintervention?

In a real sense, the Cold War is a result of the convergence of ideology and ambition such as characterized the periods before the Peace of Westphalia and the French Revolutionary–Napoleonic Wars. The Truman Doctrine and the Marshall Plan were thus elements in an increasingly global revolutionary struggle, the objective of whose combatants was not only to extend direct territorial control but also to modify political regimes and socioeconomic structures. In such a context, American support, covert and open, to liberal political forces in Western Europe was seen by the concerned public as both necessary and proper. Even the extension of assistance to regimes more authoritarian in nature was widely seen as a justifiable attempt to limit Soviet influence.

The experience of Vietnam and the political and economic costs of intervention in areas of high political instability led many opinion leaders, however, to reassess America's international role. At the same time, some

Western commentators on Soviet ambitions undertook a parallel reassessment. The convergence of these trends is most visibly seen in the détente policy of former Secretary of State Henry Kissinger.

If U.S. foreign policy since World War II has been largely inspired by polar confrontation and nation building among the noncommunist states, recent détente policy was aimed—in the words of its primary expositor, Henry Kissinger—at the encouragement of "an environment in which competitors can regulate and restrain their differences and ultimately move from competition to cooperation."[17] The primary focus of U.S. policy thus became less the containment—and, in effect, the isolation—of the Soviet Union than the development of a nexus of relations designed to "create a vested interest in cooperation and restraint."[18] And although the earlier containment doctrine largely represented a negative policy vis-à-vis the East and placed dominant emphasis on the development and maintenance of alliance ties with Western Europe, Japan, and other states of important strategic interest, the practical result of Kissinger's policy was to reverse the emphasis and increasingly assess our alliance relations in terms of their contribution to Soviet-American détente.

This approach is ultimately founded on three assumptions. First, in the words of Kissinger, "the Soviet Union has begun to practice foreign policy—at least partially—as a relationship between states rather than as international civil war";[19] in any case, common interests in survival and some degree of predictability are more important factors in U.S.-Soviet relations than basic changes in their regimes or ideological motivations. Second, a strong Western military posture and a continuing intimacy within the Western alliance will be maintained. Third, a separation between domestic and international politics and a clearer acceptance of spheres of influence in the policies of the Soviet Union and the United States can be established.

To critics who asserted that political and economic concessions by the United States to the Soviet Union should be linked to a modification of Soviet domestic policy in the areas of emigration and perhaps dissent, Kissinger replied: "Where the age-old antagonism between freedom and tyranny is concerned, we are not neutral. But other imperatives impose limits on our ability to produce internal changes in foreign countries. Consciousness of our limits is recognition of the necessity of peace—not moral callousness."[20] In effect, Kissinger contended that a stable international system thus depended on an agreement about international rules of behavior—not on a common notion of justice, which could well place in doubt the authority of the several regimes comprising the system. To attempt to devise agreements that establish both rules of international conduct and norms of domestic rectitude, he argued, is likely to increase frustration and exacerbate conflict, especially in an international environment characterized by fundamentally different regimes. At the same time, however, it is clear that Kissinger did not elevate the doctrine of nonintervention to a categorical imperative but limited it to great-power, i.e., Soviet-American, relations and coupled the notion with an implicit understanding on spheres of influence. The distinction between domestic and international politics and the concomitant rule of nonintervention are thus prudential and limited rather than principled and universal. It is not that an absolute doctrine of nonintervention is simply rejected in the abstract but that conditions of state security, as well as state aspirations, are viewed as ruling out complete submission to such a precept. Indeed, the classical notion of power politics has always distinguished between great and small powers and included concepts of spheres of influence. Inhibitions on ideological preferences and restrictions on direct interference in domestic politics arise—in this view— not from abstract notions of justice but from calculations of prudence. The latter includes, it must be noted, the elaboration of prudential rules of international behavior and guides for alliance maintenance. In this conception, then, Kissinger was not alone but part of a long and dominant foreign policy tradition.

In effect, Kissinger argued that the diverse character of the international system and the overriding interest in preventing a nuclear holocaust suggested prudence in any pursuit of global justice and greater attention to standards of interstate behavior. The role of the United States government was that of a broker attempting to induce *both* the American people and the Soviet regime to move back in the direction of the principles of Westphalia.

However, Kissinger pursued this notion so single-mindedly that the American people increasingly perceived his policy as not only uninspiring but also cynical. The only standard by which it could be admired was one of continuous success. Carter apparently grasped, responded to, and probably shared these sentiments. Whatever success the human rights campaign has had abroad, it generated spectacular popular support at home. Carter did not create the human rights impetus in the contemporary political scene—indeed, Congress preceded him and probably still outstrips him in this area—but he has benefited from the sentiment, whatever long-term strictures it may place on his flexibility. And to the degree that the conduct of foreign policy requires popular support, Carter's policy has provided him with some degree of strength, which could endure a series of setbacks in the international arena. It seems clear that a stable foreign policy consensus in this country requires an external policy sensitive to the founding principles of the republic. It may be equally true, however, that international stability requires the revival of some notion of nonintervention. The art of statesmanship lies in the balancing of these two demands.

Conclusions

U.S. foreign policy has been drawn in two directions—

toward concentration on the *effects* of other states' external behavior and toward concern for the *motivations* of such behavior, motivations that arise from the character of a state's domestic regime. Any policy must be cognizant of both dimensions, but different emphases will modify the basic thrust and the rationalizing principles of one's foreign policy.

The doctrine of containment put heavy emphasis on the ideological sources of Soviet conduct and consequently aimed not only at the restraint of the external impulse of the Soviet regime but also at the ultimate modification of the character of that regime. Critics of this perspective argued that the ideological character of the regime was less important than the balance of forces and the dangers and opportunities that the balance presented to the Soviet leadership. It was hence argued that to focus one's attention on the ideological motivations and threat of the Soviet regime could divert one's notice from the crucial geostrategic elements of one's security.

To a substantial degree, Henry Kissinger came to accept the latter commentary and further argued that it was in the interest both of the United States and the Soviet Union to concentrate less on the ideological origins and rationale for their policies. It can be argued that this perspective made him less sensitive not only to the continuing strength of ideology as a source and instrument of Soviet policy but also the continued importance to the U.S. Congress and people of a policy animated and justified by reference to the founding principles of the republic.

President Carter sensed and shared this latter concern and consequently fashioned a foreign policy impulse that brought into major key the human rights theme. At the same time, the animus that such a campaign could introduce into our relations with all communist states and the complications that would develop with noncommunist, generally friendly states—which, indeed, could be far more affected by the campaign than the communist states—suggest a note of caution concerning Carter's attention to international human rights.

Indeed, the author of the Mr. X article, George Kennan, who contends that the ideological character of his analysis has been exaggerated, has recently observed: "A certain amount of pressure on the Soviet Union is useful, too much can be self-defeating. There is a very fine line here, and I hope Carter doesn't get pushed beyond that. It's like taking pills—good in measure but dangerous in excess."[21] James Reston has concluded that Kennan is counseling the wisdom of the whale, "which is that you are more likely to get harpooned when you're up on the surface spouting too much."[22]

The revolutionary character of our era and the international position of the United States probably render impossible a simple application of John Quincy Adams's maxim; but if the human rights campaign overshadows all other strategic concerns, we may be drawn to the core of its wisdom: "We are friends of liberty everywhere but custodians only of our own."

Notes

1. *New York Times*, January 21, 1977.
2. George T. Kennan, *Russia and the West under Lenin and Stalin* (Boston: Little, Brown and Co., 1960), p. 79.
3. "The Sources of Soviet Conduct," *Foreign Affairs* 25, no. 4 (July 1947): 566-582. Reprinted in *Caging the Bear: Containment and the Cold War,* ed. Charles Gati (Indianapolis and New York: Bobbs-Merrill Co., 1974).
4. Quoted in Gati, *Caging the Bear,* p. 18.
5. Ibid., pp. 21, 22-23.
6. Walter Lippman, *The Cold War: A Study in U.S. Foreign Policy,* ed. Ronald Steel (New York: Harper and Row, 1972), p. 22.
7. Ibid., p. 26.
8. Ibid., p. 31.
9. Ibid., p. 35.

10. U.S., Department of State, Bureau of Public Affairs, Office of Media Services, News Release, March 17, 1977, p. 3.

11. Cited by Winston Lord, U.S., Department of State, Bureau of Public Affairs, Office of Media Services, News Release, November 11, 1976, p. 1.

12. Richard N. Current, ed., *The Political Thought of Abraham Lincoln* (Indianapolis and New York: Bobbs-Merrill Co., 1967), p. 12, the "Lyceum speech."

13. *New York Times*, January 21, 1977.

14. *New York Times*, February 24, 1977.

15. *Pravda*, September 25, 1968, cited in the *New York Times*, September 27, 1968.

16. V. Matreyev, *Izvestiia*, December 2, 1975, p. 4.

17. U.S., Department of State, Bureau of Public Affairs, Office of Media Services, News Release, September 19, 1974, no. 6, pp. 3-4.

18. U.S., Department of State, Bureau of Public Affairs, Office of Media Services, News Release, October 10, 1973, pp. 4-5.

19. Ibid., p. 4.

20. U.S., Department of State, Bureau of Public Affairs, Office of Media Services, News Release, September 19, 1974, no. 6, p. 3.

21. *New York Times*, February 11, 1977.

22. Ibid.

9. Internationally Diffused Innovation and Conditions of Change in Eastern Europe

Arpad Abonyi

After the end of World War II, the international diffusion of the Soviet model of social transformation brought a discernible phase of innovation to Eastern Europe, an area long known both for its lack of industrial expansion and its ardently nationalistic, conservative-authoritarian regimes. The transmission of this model mobilized and reorganized political, economic, and social values and institutions throughout the region; and it promoted the transformation of societies toward the goals of Marxism-Leninism, under the guidance and control of communist parties.

By examining the structural conditions that have characterized the diffusion and perpetuation of the Soviet model, we can analyze the conflicts surrounding innovation in the Eastern European transformation. First, we suggest that the international transmission of the model, though it represents innovation in the region, is also part of a structural relationship of inequality, a relationship in which Soviet values and institutions have been diffused and maintained regardless of national political and socioeconomic conditions. Second, we suggest that inevitable conflicts emerge from the incongruence of internationally defined norms of change and national realities. We examine the sources of such conflict and how they have generated alternative national innovation strategies for the purpose of adjusting the model. In the final section, we relate how the emergent structure of regional, political, and economic relationships has channeled various national innovation strategies—arresting Czechoslovakian reforms, impeding Hungarian ones, and incorporating East Germany's—and made them conform to regional solutions. Soviet efforts over much of the last decade have been directed to the development of policies to control and homogenize change, reinforce inequality, and preserve the Soviet model in the area—the most important example being the *Comprehensive Program* of 1971.

The Concept of Innovation and Conditions of Change

Before proceeding, it seems appropriate to clarify the concept of innovation and how it is employed in the broader framework of analysis presented here. As Professor Welsh points out in an earlier part of this volume, "innovation is a special case of change." Innovation is characterized by purposeful attempts to supplant established socioeconomic or political relationships in the social system with new policies, tasks, and objectives. This process is multidimensional and may include the emergence of new elites and institutions, as well as new beliefs, attitudes, values, and behavior in political, economic, and social relations. Ultimately, whatever dimension the process of innovation takes—whether all-encompassing or segmented—it must affect the structure and functioning of the social system.

Clearly, not all policy innovations affect the entire social system to the same degree. Two major types of innovation are discernible. In the first instance, innovation occurs at the societal level, when a society's persisting identity, "as a result of disturbances induced either by internal developments or impacts from without, changes its structural form."[1] This category of innovation closely resembles the threshold conception suggested by Welsh, for it can be studied in terms of the absolute magnitude of change away from the base line. In Eastern Europe, for example, the base line is represented by previous capitalist or "precapitalist" societies, and the absolute magnitude of change is by their transformation into Marxist-Leninist societies.

The alternative view of threshold conception offered by Welsh—that one can understand absolute change through the cumulative impact of incremental change—should be qualified when analyzing the transformation process in Eastern Europe. The notion of incremental change, which has been an extensive part of functionalist theories of international integration, implies the operation of a utilitarian calculus.[2] Change is an assumed by-product of policy space responding—through gradual, item-by-item decision making—to the forces of technical and economic rationality.[3] Moreover, these forces compete in a depoliticized environment, with subsystem autonomy often prevailing over political considerations.[4]

Whatever form it takes, innovation is subject to the forces of diffusion, which are not always autonomously produced from the internal, organic workings of society. In certain cases, as Welsh has observed, innovation is externally introduced into the recipient unit. In the Eastern European context, we might well examine this tendency from a transnational perspective based on the following set of working hypotheses: first, that innovation is more likely to be diffused from the external, international environment when societies are sensitive to transnational structures and conditions; second, that societies are more likely to be sensitive to transnational linkages and less autonomous if the sources of growth, rewards, and sustenance of their domestic organizations and processes predominantly emanate from the international environment; third, that this vulnerability, which emerges from extensive reliance on external sources, is more likely to occur in societies that have an asymmetrical distribution of attributes and values vis-à-vis other societies in the international system. These asymmetries may develop from uneven distribution of natural resources, from late and uneven industrialization. Whatever the form, asymmetries are important in the consideration of societal innovation. They reduce, to some degree, possibilities of domestically defined and directed change, i.e., autonomy, and they facilitate the infusion of external sources of innovation.

International Diffusion of Innovation and the Conditions of Socioeconomic Transformation in Eastern Europe

The diffusion of the Soviet model in Eastern Europe is the latest phase in the evolution of an area that has been particularly sensitive to realignments in the international system. This sensitivity has been historically nurtured by the region's late drive toward industrial development and by its participation in the international division of labor. For instance, a feudal aristocracy and landowning gentry dominated many Eastern European countries until the early part of this century. This socioeconomic structure promoted agrarian-based development and foreign-financed, technologically inefficient, export-oriented industrial sectors. The fragile industrial base, which was developed mainly by conservative-authoritarian regimes, suffered the onslaught of two world wars. Between the wars, the region was characterized by extreme economic nationalism, an inability to innovate, and a trade pattern that linked it as an agricultural and primary goods supplier to Western Europe in general and to Germany in particular.[5]

The experience of war and a lack of industrial expansion reinforced the region's asymmetries with the international environment. Moreover, East Europe's political and military inferiority enabled the dominant actor to emerge, namely, the Soviet Union, which imposed its model of socioeconomic transformation on the area through *penetra-*

tion and diffusion of *values* and *structures*, including the practice of economic autarky, which forced a redirection of the region's trade toward the Soviet Union. As a result, societal innovation has been part of an ongoing policy of socioeconomic mobilization in Eastern Europe since the late 1940s. The new regimes in the area have sought purposefully to transform previous societal identities and at the same time to create technologically modern economies within the confines of nationally based development strategies.

These regimes—the agents of innovation—are composed of penetrated elites in communist parties, which serve as bridgeheads for the constant transmission of Soviet interests in each East European country. In return, the penetrated elites enjoy a privileged, dominant, and hegemonic position within their own societies, a position based largely on economic, political, and military support from abroad. This exchange relationship is a structurally unequal one, in which the dominant Soviet elites are linked in a "feudal," bilateral interaction pattern to their subordinate Eastern European counterparts. This situation closely resembles the asymmetric linkage between Third World and industrialized Western capitalist countries. Indeed, Johan Galtung, who has critically analyzed linkages between Third World and Western industrialism, recently transposed his analysis to the Soviet-East European relationship.[6] Galtung describes this relationship as social imperialism, in which the Soviet center imposes a certain social structure on the Eastern European periphery. In social imperialism, according to Galtung, the center provides the model, and the periphery confirms the validity of the model; the center expands through the creation of homologous structures everywhere; and the center creates bridgeheads in order to gain leverage for the internal control of the periphery.

In Eastern Europe, then, international penetration has ensured that *societal innovation* closely conforms to Soviet political and economic structures and values. Communist parties take an ideologically prescribed leading role in the eradication of capitalism and its trappings as well as in the reorientation of society on the basis of Marxist-Leninist goals. They initiate this task through democratic centralism, in which all societal relations are subordinated in a hierarchical structure dominated by the party, which is itself composed of a narrow elite and is centrally organized.

In its leading role, the party mobilizes resources in society, converting them from private to public purposes. Through formal or informal mechanisms and relying extensively on the use of coercion, especially in the consolidation of power, it aggregates and controls interests and thereby acts as an instrument to shape the attitudes and opinions of society. Because of such central control, all aspects of social activity are politicized. Private interests, political opposition, and conflicting ideologies, which were characteristic of the previous capitalist society, are to a greater or lesser degree suppressed.

In its leading role, the party has also diffused new values to guide the transformation of society. In addition to the expropriation of private property, bourgeois elements were victimized and in some cases destroyed. Moreover, individualism and materialism were discouraged because they led to competition and inequality in both the economic and political marketplace, thereby providing an opportunity for suppression and exploitation. In place of these bourgeois values, the parties promoted the subordination of the individual's role to the greater good of the social collectivity, stressing the notion of oneness and equality in society, the common bond between workers and peasants, and their objective right to rule through the party. Most important, the party emphasized the mobilization of resources for economic development and industrialization. In the transformation toward a new, utopian society, the Leninist regimes of Eastern Europe couched their ideology in national terms, appealing to nationalist ambitions to develop an industrial collectivity and a new national identity in the context of a socialist state.

Penetration not only facilitated the diffusion of the model, but also provided important leverage through formal and informal, political and economic linkages of control between the dominant Soviet elites and their subservient East European counterparts. Each party in the region is linked bilaterally to the Communist Party of the Soviet Union (CPSU). At the outset of the transformation period, it was CPSU policy to determine the leadership and program of each East European party. The CPSU also educated and assigned instructors to party schools and central committees. The "Soviet embassy system," throughout the area, internally monitored the performance and commitment of each party to Soviet policy. Soviet ambassadors gave frequent advice to party leaders and, at Moscow's instructions, often played an important role in arranging East European economic plans to suit Soviet production objectives. To be sure, this relationship has evolved over time; it is now neither as harsh nor as directive as it once was. There has also been a movement to more formal institutions such as the Council for Mutual Economic Assistance (COMECON). However, bilateral links are still a determining force in each party's strategy, and the CPSU still retains the right to determine what constitutes an acceptable Leninist regime.

Internationally diffused innovation, then, such as that undertaken in Eastern Europe from 1950 to the early 1960s, eventually results in a paradox. Despite external penetration, national priorities cannot be totally ignored. Each communist party in the area has a declared obligation of transforming society in accord with Marxist-Leninist goals and objectives. Their ability to do so, and at the same time satisfy enough of the populace, is crucial to the stability of society as well as their own survival. They are middlemen, with dual loyalties in an unequal tug of war. The success of this type of societal innovation, therefore, rests with the penetrated elite and its ability to balance the countervailing forces within the structural contraints imposed on it.

Adaptation to National Conditions and the Emergence of Alternative Innovations

In this balancing process, East European regimes have had to respond to the sources of the societal conflicts that are an inevitable outgrowth of incongruence between internationally diffused values and structures, and particular national realities and priorities. This is not a problem particular to East Europe. It is also a concern of Third World countries, which constantly deal with the economic impact of external penetration by multinational corporations and Western demonstration effects. In dealing with the roots of societal conflicts, East European regimes have had to adapt the innovation process and generate alternative national strategies without essentially altering the principles of Marxist-Leninist societies. This process of accommodation signifies a change in the economic structure and political function of national development strategies. It also includes the absorption of new values and the emergence to prominence of new actors. Because of their unequal levels of industrial development and distribution of resources, not all Eastern European countries instituted *intrasocietal* innovation at the same time or indeed in the same way. Nevertheless, this form of innovation generally began to appear in the early 1960s.

Three related sources of societal conflicts are identifiable. The first can be characterized by the general crisis of legitimacy—the party's enduring quest for popular recognition of its authority. Popular acceptance has been thwarted for several reasons. For example, the excessive use of force in the early phase of social innovation alienated sizable portions of East European populations. On the other hand, the traditional values inherent in these societies undermine their propensity to identify on a normative plane with Marxist-Leninist values and structures, including the penetrated elite. By their very nature, socialization processes have been unable to dislodge these traditional norms. Appealing to nationalist aims and often reinforcing a historically rooted nationalism, they prompt attachments to past national identities and a sense of uniqueness. This has helped them to maintain a guarded suspicion of all things Russian and to preserve Eastern Europe's social preoccupation with tradition—the church in Poland, the unification question in East Germany, the unique Magyar heritage in the midst of a Slavic sea, the visions of previous democratic life in Czechoslovakia, and Rumania's former role as a Latin oasis in Eastern Europe.

In attacking the roots of the problem, East European regimes embarked on a new phase of accommodation. They have sought to legitimize their exercise of power through greater use of persuasion. The success of this endeavor increasingly rests upon integrating the masses and emergent technical elites into a Marxist-Leninist society. In some countries, there has been a willingness to decrease the party's active intervention in daily life in return for passive acceptance of its leading role. Such policies were a popular aspect of early Czech reforms, and are still prominent in Poland and Hungary. Relative depoliticization has not meant abandoning the goals of a Marxist-Leninist society. Rather, political indoctrination was replaced by a tangible increase in the standard of living and by real efforts at making consumer goods available. Consumerism, however, relies on adapting the economy to technological intensive development. The partial evolution of economic tasks toward such goals has required the emergence of technical elites to manage an economy of greater complexity and functional specificity.

The necessary presence and possible demands of such a new breed of counterelite poses a challenge to the penetrated strategic elite—those who control the party hierarchy. As such, this antagonism constitutes the second source of societal conflict. The emergence of these technocrats dealt the final blow to the monolithic makeup of the party and meant that there was competition for the strategic positions in the party hierarchy. People such as Mittag, Jarowinski, and Apel in East Germany, Sik in Czechoslovakia, and Nyers and Fehér in Hungary represented a more pragmatic approach to economic problem solving. Though more conservative in East Germany, these technocrats were not primarily motivated by ideology, as were the older, orthodox vanguard of their respective parties. Although recognizing the importance of ideology, the technocrats primarily promoted rationalization of the economy, although not in the same way or to the same degree. As such, they threatened to disrupt political priorities, especially those favored by hard-line factions who continued to believe that the economy was merely a branch or tool of political decision making. Nevertheless, in order to maintain their leading role in the accommodation phase, East European parties increasingly relied on institutionally controlled consultation and cooperation of these technocrats and, through them, on an armada of enterprise managers and economists.

The third point of conflict centers on how to resolve the inefficiencies of extensively based, centrally planned autarkic industrialization and on how to adopt intensive methods of economic growth. The political goals and economic requirements of the accommodation phase are intertwined. In addition to the political requisites, the need for economic rationalization within this phase is a result of the operation of the Soviet model. Expansion in the favored heavy industry sectors is realized through ever-increasing inputs of capital and labor. This unbalanced and extensive growth has become progressively less viable in Eastern Europe. As the supply of labor and natural resources decreases, more investment capital is required for increased output. Given the finite sources for quantitative growth, unless investment capital is made more productive through technological change and unless labor and managerial skills are increased, rates of output will fall while incurred costs rise exponentially. Unfortunately, this type of forced industrialization creates the need for quantitative growth. The directive nature of the planning system stifles entrepreneurship and hinders the development of new technologies and qualitative improvements in production, especially because of a lack of parametric prices for measuring costs and gains. Therefore, it becomes difficult to continue emphasis on heavy industrialization priorities, let alone shift resources into consumer industries.

In order to resolve these problems, East European regimes have resorted to various economic reforms. Radoslav Selucky has categorized them three ways: (1) administrative, (2) mixed or hybrid, and (3) market socialism. The first is the most conservative and refers to efforts at improving the command system, which is basically considered still viable. Such reform is exemplified by East Germany's New Economic System. The hybrid form, on the other hand, combines centralized macroeconomic decision making with some degree of microeconomic managerial autonomy according to market-type regulations. This continues planned direction of the economy but attempts to incorporate market efficiency into the plan. Hungary's New Economic Mechanism (NEM) is a case in point. The third category is the most radical in the East European context, for it considers central command planning as irretrievably inefficient. Under "market socialism," the plan atrophies to the point where it only ameliorates the social effects of a market-directed economy. This last type of reform, however, may mean more than a simple readjustment. It may unleash the forces that change the structural identity of a Marxist-Leninist society, as it did in Czechoslovakia. More specifically, if decision making is decentralized and prices replace planners' preferences as economic criteria, what has become of the party's leading role? Under these circumstances, nationally generated innovation exceeds the regional Soviet definition of what constitutes a Marxist-Leninist society, and structural constraints become crucial to the form and direction of innovation.

Structural Constraints: Regional Solutions to Natural Problems

The generation of these national innovation strategies in Eastern Europe represents a genuine attempt at adjusting the Soviet model of innovation to national political priorities and economic realities. Although political and economic requisites are intertwined in these alternative strategies, the common denominator for success ultimately lies in reforming the inefficiencies of the centrally planned economy. This is true especially in countries such as East Germany, Czechoslovakia, and Hungary, which inherited predictable economic difficulties due to their lack of natural resources and shortage of labor. At the same time, lest we forget, these inefficiencies have fostered a dependent structure of regional trade with the Soviet core area. The industrial growth of Eastern European countries, particularly the smaller ones, becomes tied to the expanding extraction of Soviet raw materials, in return for which they must also expand exports of machinery to the Soviet market or invest, despite tight funds, in its development.

In addition to political linkages, the confining nature of this dependent structure of regional trade severely limits the parameters of national innovation. In effect, this has discouraged domestic readjustments which have emerged in isolation from regional political and economic relationships, by arresting those that threatened the structural forms of Marxist-Leninist society, as in Czechoslovakia. Others, such as Hungary's NEM, did not immediately threaten this form, but could not be isolated from regional political and economic relations governed by conservative norms and characterized by tied economic growth, market and raw material dependence on the Soviet Union, bilateralism, and plan coordination. Because it failed to adapt the regional norms to its needs, and therefore other members' economic mechanisms, NEM could not survive. Its steady retrenchment, since 1971, was underscored with the demotion, in 1974, of two important reformers, Nyers and Fehér, and the resignation of Nyers's most ardent supporter, Premier Fock, in 1975. Since 1971, within the context of this confining structure of regional relations, there has been an attempt to resolve the inefficiencies of central planning, which are integrally linked to surmounting the problems of intensive economic development.

One readily available solution to the problems of intensive economic growth is regional imports of Western technology, which do not threaten East European structures or relations as long as they remain a *less significant* element in a more elaborate regional strategy. These imports have been viewed as a mixed blessing by the Soviet and East European strategic elites. On the one hand, Western technology is desired to augment the deficiencies of centrally planned economies. On the other, the effective use of Western technology may require use of Western experts and their entrepreneurial or managerial skills, which may have a considerable "demonstration effect." It could strengthen the forces for change that threaten to undermine the leading role of the party. A more immediate negative consequence is that Western technology imports exacerbate Eastern Europe's already unfavorable balance of trade with Western hard-currency markets.

A far more preferable solution, economically and politically, is the creation of regionally based technologies that would augment national deficiencies and help resolve problems of intensive development. Because this type of solution can be realized in the framework of a long-range strategy, it does not pose an automatic impediment to

Western technology imports. Indeed, these imports are required to facilitate the emergence of a regional strategy by resolving some of the immediate problems of centrally planned economies. Lest this dependence be overstressed, the creation of a regional strategy is also a drive toward technological autonomy. Hence, it is meant to ensure that Western technology imports will not critically constrain the orientation of the area's future development.

A common regional economic strategy could promote "internationalization of the forces of production," which refers primarily to international division of labor, pooling of research and development efforts, and reaping economies of scale on a regional level. Given the relationships in the region, however, the resulting structural changes in patterns of production and trade may well be unequally distributed and enhance the role of the penetrating actor.

These convictions seem to be well founded. Since there are no regional market forces, foreign trade in these centrally planned economies is part of a bilateral balancing process. Thus a regional strategy would be most likely accommodated within the confines of a common regional plan, one that increasingly requires common administrative structures. Because of the direction of dependence in the area, it would be logical to assume that the Soviet Union will set the pattern for these structures and in the process attempt to preserve the identity of its internationally diffused model. This is made possible by the fact that, unlike most East European countries, the Soviet core is better able to bear the increased costs of maintaining the old command planned system without resorting to significant reorganization. Therefore, the adoption of a regional economic strategy will restrict the alternative, nationally generated innovations to conservative-administrative reforms at best.

Conclusion

The analysis presented here outlines the conditions

governing innovation in Eastern Europe since World War II. It is based on the following observations. First, historically rooted asymmetries in the area originally facilitated the international diffusion of innovation in the form of the Soviet model of socioeconomic transformation. These asymmetries also helped to develop regional political and economic relationships in which the dominant Soviet elite has been able to define the parameters of innovation. In formulating this regional definition, however, they have been insensitive to Eastern European national priorities and realities. In fact, national concerns in the area have had to be subordinated to Soviet goals and objectives.

Second, as a result of this incongruity, inevitable conflicts emerge that imply that change must satisfy national requisites. These conflicts are generated by domestic pressures to which the penetrated elites are sensitive. Indeed, if East European societies are to remain stable and if the penetrated elites are to survive, then they must reconcile internationally diffused innovation with national priorities.

Third, such attempts have been undertaken by East European regimes since the early 1960s with the generation of national innovation strategies. These strategies are part of adaptation processes that take place within the context of Marxism-Leninism. However, because of the structure of dependence in the region, the decision making freedom of nation elites is considerably curtailed. Nationally generated innovation strategies cannot exceed the boundaries defined by the dominant Soviet elite. The types of strategies that even remotely threaten the Marxist-Leninist identity of society are circumvented.

Finally, the emphasis on regional conformity is underscored by the policies promoted through the *Comprehensive Program*. The stress on conformity does not rule out innovation. It provides for domestic adaptation processes by finding regional solutions to national problems.

Notes

1. Robert Nisbet, "Introduction: The Problem of Social Change," in *Social Change,* ed. Robert Nisbet (New York: Harper and Row, 1972), p. 14.
2. See Ernst B. Haas, "Turbulent Fields and the Theory of Regional Integration," *International Organization* 30 (Spring 1976): 173-213; Charles C. Pentland, "Neofunctionalism," *The Year Book on World Affairs 1973* (London, Stevens & Sons, 1973), pp. 358-364; and Lynn Mytelka, "The Salience of Gains in Third World Integration Systems," *World Politics* 25 (January 1973): 236-250.
3. Haas, "Turbulent Fields," p. 176.
4. Pentland, "Neofunctionalism," pp. 361-362.
5. See Ivan T. Berend and György Ránki, *Economic Development in East-Central Europe in the 19th and 20th Centuries* (New York: Columbia University Press, 1974); and John Michael Montias, "Economic Nationalism in Eastern Europe: Forty Years of Continuity and Change," *Journal of International Affairs* 20 (1966): 45-71.
6. Johan Galtung, "Conflict on a Global Scale: Social Imperialism and Sub-Imperialism—Continuities in Structural Theory of Imperialism," *World Development* 4 (March 1976): 153-165.

10. Eastern Europe and Eurocommunism as Indicators of Soviet Change

Peter C. Ludz

CPSU strategies and tactics toward the West European communist parties,[1] dating back to Comintern and Cominform policies, reveal that the Soviet Union has become a superpower. Now as before, on old and new grounds, CPSU leaders claim more or less recklessly that the communist parties of all other countries recognize Soviet supremacy. On the other hand, the leadership of the Communist Party of the Soviet Union (CPSU) has to go with the times. It has to acknowledge that there exist "antagonisms" between "revolutionary" supremacy and superpower politics (détente). Such antagonisms require constant balancing and, in Soviet relationships with Eurocommunism, constant explaining. The West European parties' demands for explanation intensified after the Soviet Union signed the Final Act of Helsinki and after President Carter launched the human rights campaign.

To meet the challenges of Eurocommunism, the Soviet Union has displayed different actions and responses. Most of them stem from its defensive policies; others follow from offensive strategies. Only a few may be called cooperative. Frequently combinations of defensive, offensive, and cooperative policy measures have been applied. They have changed with the course of time; they have varied from country to country, from party to party.

The actions and responses of the CPSU leadership vis-à-vis Eurocommunism are usually the result of a complex set of evaluations and considerations. For analytical purposes, this complexity may be disentangled by differentiating between six areas of evaluation and concern:

1. Eurocommunism within the context of Western Europe, which encompasses the general assessment of capitalism, or more precisely of the political, social, and economic development of the capitalist industrial nations.
2. Eurocommunism within the context of NATO and the Atlantic Alliance, which includes USSR-U.S. relations and U.S. reactions to Eurocommunism.
3. The impact of ideas and actions of the French and Italian communist parties on domestic affairs in the Soviet Union.
4. The impact of Eurocommunist ideas and actions on the East and Southeast European communist parties, which the Soviets regard as belonging to their sphere of influence.
5. The impact of Eurocommunism on the status quo of the world communist movement.
6. The impact of Eurocommunism on the status quo of the international system or on world politics.

In contrast to the CPSU, the other East European communist parties have different priorities when evaluating Eurocommunism and deciding on actions. They all orient themselves by the Soviet line, some as followers, others as dissidents of various degrees. In addition, some East European party leaders—especially those in Yugoslavia, Poland, and Hungary—base their responses toward Eurocommunism on an evaluation of national requirements, on the political conditions and possibilities of their own countries. Their attitude is further shaped by specific real or ideological contacts with the centers of Eurocommunism in Rome, Madrid, and Paris. Thus, analytically and empirically, the Soviet response to Eurocommunism has to be distinguished from those of the East European communist parties.

What Is Eurocommunism?

"Eurocommunism," "reform communism," or "autonomous communism"[2] has a split "self-understanding," one self being presented to the West, another to the East. Whether this is a characteristic inherent in the nature of Eurocommunism or whether it is the result of specific strategic and tactical decisions by the party leaders shall not be examined here. Rather, my task is to describe those two "images" of Eurocommunism and to point out some similarities and differences between the two strands.

The self-image presented to the East puts particular emphasis on the crisis of capitalism and democracy. At their last meeting in Madrid (March 1977), the Eurocommunist leaders nearly unanimously demanded an extension of democratic processes by postulating the democratic participation of the masses. They stipulate that democracy develop into socialism. In their view, socialization of the means of production, on which the Soviet political system is based, provides an economic order that "concerning some major aspects, is superior to the capitalist market economies."[3] Emphasis on solidarity with the CPSU and the other ruling communist parties is another characteristic of the Eastern-oriented image as it emerged at both the Madrid meeting and the East Berlin Conference of June 1976. However, this tendency is combined with the search for national independence, equality of rights, mutual respect, and nonintervention.

In what may be called their Western self-image, the Eurocommunists profess their loyalty to the parliamentary democracies and the "bourgeois" freedoms. The "new society" they seek to establish is said to be based on the principles of toleration and pluralism, on the granting of individual and collective liberties. The freedoms of thought and of speech, the freedoms of the press and of assembly, the rights to strike and to protest are declared to be guaranteed. Under Eurocommunism, trade unions would keep their independence, and the principles of free and general elections would be respected, i.e., the institutionalized change of rule in democratic systems would not be jeopardized.[4]

Such affirmations ought to be followed by deeds. But so far the PCF and the PCI have refrained from reforming their own party structures by introducing democratic principles. Now as before, the PCF organization has Stalinist features, and the PCI may at best be called a party of the Leninist type. In other words, Eurocommunism still has to prove its credibility to the West by making organizational changes in the existing party apparatuses. At the same time, however, the Eurocommunist parties are undergoing ideological changes. The pressure for such changes comes from the noncommunist world, especially from the historical experience that democratic systems have been strong enough to resist all the challenges of Soviet-type communism.

The Eurocommunist self-understanding implies a clear rejection of some basic principles of the Marxist-Leninist ideology. Thus, to gain credibility in the West, the Eurocommunists could not just repeat their claim that each communist party be free in applying the teachings of Marxism-Leninism according to its national traditions. They had to become more specific, and, to a certain extent, they have done so. The "dictatorship of the proletariat" was excised from official PCF language, and the idea of monopolistic power—in both foreign and domestic affairs— was rejected.[5] In practical politics, the Eurocommunists emphasize a broad coalition of political forces (including social democratic and socialist parties) as the best way to solve the pressing political, social, and economic problems in the advanced industrial societies. They suggest this method for the present situation in Italy and, to a certain degree, in France; but they carefully avoid confusing it with Stalin's concept of the "popular front."[6]

If we compare these two images, we can note similarities as well as differences. Both the Western-oriented and the Eastern-oriented self-interpretations include such demands as independence from Soviet domination, *policentrismo* (i.e., the creation of new centers of communism), pluralism, and the preservation of the achievements of bourgeois democracy, although they do so to a different extent. However, Eurocommunists provide different treatments of themes familiar to Western audiences on the one hand and to those of the East on the other. Thus statements meant for Western consumption soften all references to the "crisis of capitalism" and solidarity with the CPSU. For the East on the other hand, the Eurocommunists play down or disguise important aspects of their Western-oriented analyses, such as their openness toward the social democratic and the socialist parties.

The political implications of this split self-understanding are as yet difficult to perceive. But given its ambivalence, Eurocommunism is more likely to be mistrusted than trusted by both the West and the East.

Major Components of Eurocommunism from the CPSU Vantage Point

What are the Soviet leaders' perceptions of Eurocommunism? More and more the rulers in the Kremlin seem to have realized that their traditional policy—namely, to push for stage-by-stage "democratic" transitions in Western Europe—has little chance of success. They have therefore increasingly valued defensive strategies. This does not mean that the Soviets would not take any offensive action. In

Sweden and Greece, they have split the communist parties, and they are trying to do the same in Spain by backing Enrique Lister against Carrillo. In the Spanish case, however, they may have been ill-advised. It seems doubtful that they will succeed in getting Carrillo under control by this policy.

In principle, the Soviets reject all tendencies of political emancipation and of autonomy among the West European communist parties. They also oppose those tendencies in the PCI, the PCF, and the PCE that result in "political reformism" and "regionalism."[7] Trends toward "autonomism," reformism and regionalism (which, in the last result, may lead to a schism of communism in Europe) are perceived by the Soviet leaders as risks to their own system of rule.

The Eurocommunists' claim to acknowledge the basic political rights—those the bourgeois emancipatory movements fought for in the nineteenth century—constitutes a major risk for the Soviet leaders. This claim has received additional strength from President Carter's human rights campaign. Ideological strategists in the Soviet Union of the Arbatov type may accentuate the domestic functions of Carter's campaign for the United States, but they cannot disguise the fact that this policy has heightened fears in the Kremlin. The Soviet leaders perceive the human rights issue as an outcome of the dual policy advocated by Zbigniew Brzezinski and William E. Griffith since 1961.[8] Dual policy, as expressed by Brzezinski again and again, means that the United States and the USSR should cooperate but, nevertheless, continue to engage in ideological confrontation. The explicitly stated goal of this policy is to help the East European states gain more independence from Moscow and thus to break up the Soviet bloc. The dual policy with its emphasis on human rights touches a sore point with Soviet ideologues. Brzezinski has included in his ideological crusade a well-grounded criticism of Soviet communism. He identifies Soviet communism as a "conservative bureaucratic doctrine," which has lost its humanism to "ideological rigidity" and "revolutionary symbolism."[9]

Brzezinski, certainly no Eurocommunist himself, has thus expressed a critique of the Soviet system of rule that will not remain unnoticed in Eastern Europe. Its effects multiply when combined with similar arguments and opinions from the Eurocommunist camp. The best example to refer to in this context is Santiago Carrillo's position. He usually does not put so much emphasis on the "different" roads toward socialism or communism, but he criticizes the Soviet road as such. This is partly why the Soviets attack Carrillo much more heavily than Berlinguer and Marchais.

The Soviet leaders perceive another risk in the contacts between the Eurocommunist parties and socialist or social democratic groupings in Western and Northern Europe. The communists in Western Europe may have different attitudes toward social democracy. But in general, they seem to agree among themselves and to disagree with the CPSU: regardless of its present state, the German Social Democratic Party is considered the political formation that has brought the bourgeois revolutions to completion. More and more the ideological leaders of the European communist parties recognize that the German Social Democrats contributed decisively to progress in social welfare matters and to the growth of the workers' movement. Therefore, the leading circles of the PCI (if not the mid-level cadres and the masses) have been staying away from a vigorous application of Stalin's doctrine that claims the "identity in character" of fascism and social democracy. And they have done away with other remnants of Stalinism. Compared with the PCI, the PCF is less advanced in its detachment from this and other components of the Stalinist heritage.

Thus, it is democratic pluralism in combination with clearly expressed anti-Stalinism that the Soviet leaders perceive as a major challenge of Eurocommunism. This perception must be viewed against the background of reemerging neo-Stalinist tendencies in the Soviet Union.[10] Only then can the full scope of Soviet fears be realized.

When evaluating the "autonomism" and "reformism" of the communist parties in the West, the Soviet leading elites perceive a third risk, i.e., the undermining of the authority of Marxism-Leninism. They are particularly worried about the growing awareness in PCI, PCF, and PCE circles that socialization and nationalization of the means of production, as carried out in the Soviet Union and in other East European communist states, have not resulted in the development of democratic political institutions. Eurocommunists in Italy, Spain, France, and Yugoslavia state more and more openly that, contrary to the postulates of Marxism-Leninism, the revolution by the proletariat in the Soviet Union has not led to a more humane way of life. On the contrary. In the Soviet Union, they complain, the centralized state is the mightiest institution, with bureaucratization and alienation determining the people's everyday lives. This challenge by Eurocommunism, which aims at the core dogma of Marxism-Leninism, should not be underestimated, even though it is hard to determine its exact political impact.

On the whole, the CPSU leaders conceive of Eurocommunism as a rather diffuse threat. More precisely, the fact that they cannot directly control the Western European movements that advocate Eurocommunism leads the Soviets to the assumption that Eurocommunism endangers the status quo in Europe and their own hegemony over East Europe. It may well be that with such perceptions the rulers in the Kremlin have become victims of the propaganda machine they themselves set in motion against Eurocommunism.

Be that as it may, Soviet perceptions of the risks of Eurocommunism are part of the present political scenery. They have an impact not only on CPSU-Eurocommunist relations, but also on European and world politics.

The CPSU and the PCF

Space will not permit a full discussion of all past and present actions and responses of the CPSU leaders vis-à-vis every individual Eurocommunist movement. I shall therefore concentrate on the French case to demonstrate the complexity of the CPSU's policy toward Eurocommunism. But before doing so, a note of caution seems appropriate. Owing to the lack of reliable data, the actual politics of the CPSU toward the Eurocommunist parties are not easily susceptible to analysis. In analyses of actual politics, the lack of detailed knowledge affects the methodology, as all students of communism know. Informed guesses often have to replace factual knowledge. This is especially true for such a multidimensional question as CPSU-Eurocommunist relations.

The French Communist Party (headed by Georges Marchais) has always had better relations with the CPSU than the Italian Communist Party (Enrico Berlinguer) or the Spanish Communist Party (Santiago Carrillo) have had. Very slowly and only recently has Marchais thrown some superfluous ideological baggage overboard. He had to do so in view of the French domestic situation and the PCF's alliance with François Mitterrand's *Parti Socialiste* (PS). The term *dictatorship of the proletariat* was eliminated from the official PCF vocabulary, and occasionally the Soviet Union was criticized for a case of human rights violation. From time to time (especially in November 1975[11]), influences from the PCI on the PCF could also be noticed.

On the other hand, particularly in recent months, Marchais has clearly retreated from his alliance with Mitterrand. He renounced his goal of partnership between Communists and Socialists, and he left the *Union de Gauche* (Alliance of the Left). At the same time, tendencies of a "patriotic communism," of a "Gaullism of the Left," have increased in the French Communist Party.

The CPSU has certainly watched Marchais's strategies

with great care, trying to influence them whenever possible. However, certain tensions between the two parties should not be overlooked. They were revealed through minor incidents. At the Twenty-Second PCF Congress in 1976, which, because of the renunciation of the "dictatorship of the proletariat," became known as a "historic" event, the Soviet Union kept a low profile. Furthermore, when Brezhnev visited France in 1977, he apparently did not contact Marchais, and Marchais did not go to Moscow for the celebrations of the sixtieth anniversary of the October Revolution. Tensions can also be detected in statements by prominent French party intellectuals, who charge the Soviets with faulty perceptions. Are the Soviets, they ask, incapable of discriminating between their true friends and their enemies?[12]

However, there are also indications that the Kremlin, now as before, has a strong and effective hold over the PCF. Apparently, the Soviet leaders have decided to follow a safe course and to make the best of the situation as it currently exists. They attempt to use the French Communists for their own goals, i.e., they count on them as a factor that may interfere with the West European and the Atlantic alliances. This is true even though the Kremlin has not directly intervened in French party affairs and even though the Soviet leaders have not cut down their criticism of the French comrades.

The evidence suggests that Moscow has never fully put its trust in the Alliance of the Left. It seems likely that the Kremlin rather early recognized traces of opportunism in Mitterrand's political character and also noticed the lack of clear-cut statements in the PS program. In addition, it may have been disturbed by the PS's variety of concepts on foreign and defense policies and on social policy. When the disintegration of the Alliance of the Left and the increasing power of the PS became apparent, the Soviets probably decided to urge retreat from the Alliance of the Left upon the PCF. Neither the Soviet leaders nor, as a matter of fact, the French Communists were willing to see the PCF forced into the role of a junior partner to the PS. Certain fears existed in both parties, namely, that Mitterrand's "social democratism" might spread, affect the PCF masses, and make them lose their identity.

What would the Kremlin gain if the Left were victorious and an alliance of PCF and PS forces seized power? Very little. The Soviet Union would not profit from a politically and economically destabilized France. On the contrary, Soviet interests would be severely hurt, for example, by an unstable economic situation caused by a flight of capital. France is an important foreign partner of the Soviet Union, especially when the political and economic influence of the U.S.-backed Federal Republic of Germany is taken into account.

The PCF's decision to retreat and thus to maintain the party traditions was not without logic. Tradition here may be described in terms of the following attitudes: anticapitalistic, anti-German, pro-Moscow, and patriotic. In this case, the French decision clearly coincided with hopes and wishes in the CPSU Politburo. Even certain patriotic and nationalist tendencies in the French Communist Party could be perceived as strengthening the Soviet international position, since the leftist Gaullism of PCF origin opposes NATO and the stationing of U.S. military forces in Europe and since it opposes the West German *Bundeswehr* and the political unification of the European states.

For the moment, in other words, CPSU and PCF interests converge. Both parties struggle against the same enemies, and both agree about certain issues, such as the recognition of the Soviet Union's superiority in world communism and the need for socialization of industries in France.

Responses of the East European Communist Parties

As stated earlier, perceptions of Eurocommunism by the

East European communist parties have a focus that differs from that of the CPSU. For the East European communist leaders, Soviet perceptions and policies provide the overall frame of reference within which specific responses to Eurocommunism exist.

Among the East European parties under Soviet influence, two groups may be distinguished: those whose political and ideological leaders are ambivalent toward Eurocommunism and those whose deviation from the Soviet position is at most marginal. The communist parties of Poland, Hungary, and, to a certain degree, Rumania, belong to the first group. Although their leaders watch developments in France and Italy with great interest and even sympathy, they refrain from clear public statements on behalf of Eurocommunism. The communist parties of Czechoslovakia, Bulgaria, and the German Democratic Republic (GDR) form the second group.[13]

Yugoslavia plays a special role. It has been a prototype in matters of Eurocommunism. It performed this role, however, long before Eurocommunism came into being. Yugoslavia has always been a center of anti-Stalinism. Its philosophers and social scientists have long criticized the Soviet system for its bureaucratism, have long pointed to alienation in the Soviet Union, and have long attacked the rigidity of Soviet Marxism-Leninism. Present Eurocommunism greatly draws on Yugoslav thought and social science analysis. Thus Yugoslavia is very close to Eurocommunism; but, on the other hand, it is ruled by a communist party. As a ruling communist party, the Yugoslav League of Communists has relations with the CPSU different from those of Eurocommunists.

The "ambivalent" East European communist parties typically fear Eurocommunism less than the hard-liners do. For example, Polish leaders have established contacts with Eurocommunist and social democratic parties. Quite a few Polish communists may consider Eurocommunism in Italy and Spain as a political movement that might be helpful in their own struggle against Soviet hegemonic claims.

The hard-liners, on the other hand, are more likely to view Eurocommunism as a threat to their own rule. In Czechoslovakia, for instance, Eurocommunism is identified with any kind of opposition to the existing government. This, of course, may be explained by the fact that the ruling elites in Czechoslovakia perceive Eurocommunism as the representative of those natural political forces that the Soviet tanks silenced in 1968. Since then the Italian and Spanish Eurocommunists have kept the memories of 1968 alive. They have published articles by pre-1968 Czechoslovak CP functionaries, thus causing constant annoyance to the present rulers in Czechoslovakia.

East Germany is a different case. Here Eurocommunism seems to be perceived particularly as an ideological and cultural challenge. But despite a general hostility, there are indications that—for tactical or other reasons—the party has made concessions to it now and then. At the end of 1976, for example, the Socialist Unity Party of East Germany (SED) published the first textbook of Marxism-Leninism written by East German philosophers and ideologues.[14] This work differs from Soviet textbooks on the same subject in that it includes extensive references and in some cases intensive discussions and intelligent critiques of Western political and social science. The range extends from the Frankfurt School (Adorno, Horkheimer, Marcuse, Habermas) on the one end to Teilhard de Chardin from the Club of Rome and Erich Fromm of the United States on the other. Raymond Aron, Zbigniew Brzezinski, Samuel P. Huntington, Alfred G. Meyer are considered as worthy of treatment as Jean-Paul Sartre and Maurice Merleau-Ponty. The textbook points to a feature of considerable political impact. By adopting concepts or ideas from Western philosophy and social science, the authors made corrections in the Marxist-Leninist dogma and—in a development without precedent—their corrections were allowed to appear in an official textbook. Thus the doctrine of the "driving forces" in history is treated in a refined way, and the "increasing role of the subjective factor" in socialist societies of the developed type receives rather unusual acknowledgment.

As these remarks demonstrate, the perceptions of Eurocommunism in East Europe vary with national conditions, and actions and responses differ from country to country. However, in each East European communist party, the attitude toward Eurocommunism is an indicator of the degree to which the country depends on the Soviet Union or strives for autonomy.

Influences of Eurocommunism on Eastern Europe

In view of the broad spectrum of defensive measures applied by the CPSU against Eurocommunism, it is legitimate to ask whether the Eurocommunists have a real chance to influence national politics in Eastern Europe. This question, however, should be preceded by another one: do the Eurocommunist leaders actually want to exert influence in Eastern Europe, and do they concern themselves with the affairs of individual East European countries? A definitive answer to this question is not possible. Despite the existing net of West-West and West-East communications among the communist parties, we can observe certain tendencies of national isolation among the Eurocommunists. As Carrillo, asked about the Eurocommunists' anti-Sovietism, put it, "We are not defining ourselves by taking a negative position toward others."[15] In other words, Eurocommunists refuse either to accept the Soviet practice of interference in the affairs of other parties and nations or to adopt a similar policy.

However, even if the Eurocommunists do not wish to exert any influence on East European national politics, they do have a kind of de facto power. Eurocommunism undoubtedly sharpens the crisis of legitimacy in the Soviet Union and in other East European countries.

It is not surprising, therefore, that some observers in the West relate the Soviet attitude toward Eurocommunism to domestic problems in the Soviet Union and Eastern Europe. They argue that the Soviet Union and the East European countries are affected by some kind of internal unrest, and that the Soviet Union therefore tries to bar all influences of Eurocommunism. Western analysts base this evaluation on the following evidence: an unresolved problem of nationalism in the Soviet Union, the trouble caused by dissidents in the Soviet Union and other East European countries, the lack of work enthusiasm in the Eastern bloc societies, the atractiveness of the Western style of life, the decline in motivation among the younger generation, and the diminishing possibilities of winning the young over to the ideological dogma of Marxism-Leninism.

At this point, it is easier to raise clear questions than answer them. One such question is: do the Eurocommunist party leaders and intellectuals have any chance at all to change sociopolitical conditions in Eastern Europe and thus make life easier for the people living there? In this respect, let us note the talks with Eurocommunist leaders that took place behind closed doors in Poland, Yugoslavia, Rumania, as well as the Soviet Union. As for Poland, these talks seem to have had some effect: tendencies toward further relaxation of controls and an effort on the part of the party to extend the individual's scope may be observed. The distribution of Western publications in the East or radio broadcasts might also be ways to influence East European and Soviet sociopolitical conditions. But who would be reached by these means? And the existing stations, i.e., the Voice of America and Radio Free Europe/Radio Liberty—although heard by millions of people in Eastern Europe—can hardly be called proper instruments of Eurocommunism. Eurocommunism in Eastern Europe faces a certain dilemma: its critique of conditions in East European societies often cannot be separated from criticism launched by outspoken anticommunists. Thus, on many occasions, the party propaganda easily disposed of Eurocommunist arguments, since it was able to denounce them as "reactionary," inspired by "bourgeois backwardness," or "imperialist middlemen."

The Eurocommunists' perceptions of the general international situation and the specific internal conditions in some individual countries of Eastern Europe also raise important problems: namely, what international conditions and what domestic state of affairs allow certain ideological perspectives to become effective among specific elites or the masses? And finally what are the adequate forms of influence?

To answer these questions, one would have to have a clear knowledge of the socioeconomic and sociopolitical situation, the discontent of the masses, the possibilities of free information, and existing social mechanisms (particularly those that individuals or groups can use to resist the state). Do Eurocommunist leaders, ideologues, and the party-bound sociologists and political scientists really have such knowledge? A careful investigation would probably reveal a rather alarming ignorance among the West European communist functionaries about the actual situation and aspirations of the masses in the Soviet Union and in Eastern Europe. The literature authorized by the party centers demonstrates that ideological-dogmatic problems, i.e., the search for the right combination between criticism of and solidarity with the Soviet Union, outweigh all other concerns.[16]

Finally, mention should be made of the arguments that stress the differences between the political cultures in the West and the East. Many an intellectual in East Berlin or Warsaw, in Prague or Budapest, may be attracted by Western spirit and culture, but the political culture that has been forced upon Eastern Europe for the past thirty years has certainly developed habits of its own. We are not aware of the extent of such new tendencies, especially among different social strata, but it is plausible to assume that they do exist. Thus in Eastern Europe Eurocommunism, in ideological and political terms, confronts audiences that may be quite different from its audiences in the West.

Summary

Apparently Eurocommunism presents a threat to the Communist Party of the Soviet Union, but in the West we lack detailed knowledge about Soviet perceptions. This makes an evaluation difficult; on the other hand, it stimulates speculation. Thus there is a variety of propositions and prognoses about Eurocommunism, the CPSU, and Eastern Europe. Charles Gati has formulated the thesis of the "Europeanization of Eurocommunism."[17] He identifies economic difficulties and the lack of legitimacy resulting from the communist party monopoly of decision making and the subordination of national aims to the Soviet Union as major problems facing the East European communist leaders. The adoption of certain features of Eurocommunism, he argues, namely, a broader sharing of responsibility for decision making, would provide plausible solutions to these problems.

In my view the picture Gati paints is abstract and too optimistic. He overlooks certain aspects of the situation and some of the actual problems in Eastern Europe. There is no doubt that the CPSU leaders have been winning back their control. In March and April 1977, international East bloc conferences severely affected the attitude toward Eurocommunism held by Polish, Hungarian, and Rumanian communist party leaders. Since the summer of 1977, Eurocommunism has been officially condemned and denounced as anti-Soviet by all East European communist parties, with the exception of the Yugoslav Party.

Of course, Soviet control over Eastern Europe is not total. At the summit meeting in East Berlin in June 1976, the Soviets had to moderate their demands. Several of the claims they established during the period 1974-76 had to be given up by 1976: acknowledgment that the guiding center of world communism is Moscow; acceptance of the Soviet model of dealing with the West European states and with various sociopolitical groups within those states; acceptance of the Soviet interpretation of "socialism" and "democracy"; recommendation of East European socialism/communism as a model for the development of West European communism; a favorable evaluation of the policy of the Portuguese communists; and the banning of Maoism and the policy of Communist China.

Compared with these compromises, Brezhnev's gains are meager. But it is wrong to assume that the CPSU has been defeated, even if—ideologically, not politically—it has been pushed into a defensive position by Eurocommunism and the worldwide outcry for basic human rights.

Notes

1. The term *Eurocommunism* refers here and in the following to the communist parties of Italy (Partito Comunista Italiano, or PCI), France (Parti Communiste Français, or PCF), and Spain (Partido Comunista de España, or PCE). The Yugoslav and other brands of Eurocommunism will be mentioned expressly, if necessary.

2. A valuable attempt to define Eurocommunism adequately can be found in Kurt Seliger, "Eurokommunismus im Zweispalt," *Osteuropa* 27, no. 10 (October 1977): 848-859.

3. Enrico Berlinguer in *Il compromesso storico*, ed. Pietro Valenza (Rome: Newton Compton, 1975).

4. See the Madrid Declaration, *Neues Deutschland*, March 4, 1977, p. 6. For a general evaluation of the Madrid meeting, see James O. Goldsborough, "Eurocommunism after Madrid," *Foreign Affairs* 55, no. 7 (July 1977): 800-814.

5. For the ideological and political development in the PCF, see Jean Kanapa, "A New Policy of the French Communists?" *Foreign Affairs* 55, no. 2 (January 1977): 280-294.

6. For this specific aspect, see Charles Gati, "The 'Europeanization' of Communism." *Foreign Affairs* 55, no. 3 (April 1977): 541-542.

7. William E. Griffith, "'Eurocommunism': The Third Great Communist Schism?" (Paper distributed by the Center for International Studies of the Massachusetts Institute of Technology, Cambridge, November 8, 1976).

8. Zbigniew Brzezinski and William E. Griffith, "Peaceful Engagement in Eastern Europe," *Foreign Affairs* 39, no. 4 (July 1961).

9. Zbigniew Brzezinski, *Between Two Ages: America's Role in the Technetronic Era* (New York: The Viking Press, 1970), pp. 123 ff.

10. One of the many recent testimonies to these developments is the open letter to Leonid Brezhnev by Boris Rabot, published in November 1977: "You [Leonid Ilyich Brezhnev] wanted to bring about order and discipline after Khrushchev's 'chaos' and 'disorder;' instead, dissidents crop up like mushrooms after the rain. You wanted to reassert control of the international Communist movement; instead you find yourself sandwiched between the Chinese heresy and the challenge of Eurocommunism. You wanted to stabilize relations with the West and fend off old-fashioned Stalinist excesses at home; instead, your détente policy is falling apart and you are presiding over a drift to neo-Stalinism." *New York Times Magazine,* November 6, 1977, p. 48. Boris Rabot is a former secretary of the Social Science Section of the Presidium of the USSR Academy of Sciences and an adviser to the Central Committee of the CPSU.

11. The November 1975 convergence of the Italian and the French communists was rather hectic; it was not the result of a slow and sound development.

12. Jean Elleinstein, *Le P.C.* (Paris: Bernard Gassett, 1976), p. 36. Elleinstein is the deputy director of the Centre d'Etudes et de Recherches Marxistes and a member of the French Communist Party.

13. At least, the communist parties of Czechoslovakia, Bulgaria, and East Germany have not shown any signs of restraint concerning the Soviet line toward Eurocommunism, and on many occasions they have backed the Soviets wholeheartedly. In the case of the SED, however, an interesting detail should be mentioned here. The SED was the only ruling communist party in Eastern Europe that allowed the CSCE Final Act to be published in full. *Neues Deutschland* was again the only party paper to print all the speeches given at the summit meeting of the European communist parties in East Berlin (June 1976) and to publish the Madrid Declaration of the PCE, the PCF, and the PCI (March 1977).

14. Institut für Gesellschaftswissenschaften beim ZK der SED, *Grundlagen des historischen Materialismus* (Berlin: Dietz Verlag, 1976).

15. Quoted from J. O. Goldsborough, "Eurocommunism after Madrid," p. 813.

16. For example, Jean Elleinstein, *L'Histoire du phénomène stalinien* (Paris: Grasset et Fasqualle, 1975); or Pierre Daix, *Marxismus: Die Doktrin des Terrors* (Graz, Austria, 1976).

17. Charles Gati, "The 'Europeanization' of Communism?"

11. The Kremlin and Problems of Innovation

Dan N. Jacobs

No discussion of innovation in the USSR—by *innovation* is meant purposely induced significant change either in policy or in bureaucratic structure—can be complete without consideration of the role of the Politburo (PB) of the Communist Party of the Soviet Union (CPSU) in that process.

For many years, students of the Soviet Union—and even some contemporary specialists—have tended to regard the PB as the only source of innovation in the Soviet system. Nothing could be accomplished without it. In more recent years, however, many scholars have demonstrated how simplistic it is not to recognize that there are actual and potential sources of authority and innovation other than the PB. Any number of studies have indicated the role of the party leadership at levels lower than the PB, the role of the military, the technical bureaucracy, and the scientific community in determining the activities of the party and government. In some instances, the importance of such groups has been so emphasized as to create the impression that the PB is itself besieged and incapable of initiative except as others permit it to move.

The latter would seem to be a caricature of the actual

situation. For the entire Soviet epoch, the PB has been the preeminent source of innovation in the USSR, and although its potential for innovation has been trimmed by the advent of a more complex economy and society, it continues to have the greatest potential for innovation of any group or institution in the Soviet system. In practice, any initiative, if it is to be long maintained or widely diffused, if it does not indeed originate with the PB, must have the latter's approval or *acquiescence* at a relatively early date.

There have been two major innovational periods in the history of the Soviet Union. One of these is roughly 1927-1932, the other 1957-1962.

Should the Lenin period also be included as a major innovational episode? By definition, after all, a social revolution is innovative. And certainly, new institutions such as the Comintern were created, and a qualitatively different atmosphere appeared in some areas of Russian life. By this token, innovation occurred under Lenin. However, there would seem to be two good reasons to exclude those early post-Revolution years. First, the type of innovation being considered here is the type that significantly changes an ongoing system. It does not involve innovation surrounding the seizure of power. Second, most of Lenin's activity was directed toward giving a Bolshevik cast to *existing* institutions. The extent to which Lenin made use of the surviving tsarist apparatus in order to cement Bolshevik power is well documented. Most of Lenin's activity was, of necessity, a rescue operation. Attempting to hold the power seized in the face of ubiquitous and persistent opposition, he did not, after the initial seizure of power, direct his major efforts toward innovation.

The first innovational period (1927-1932) occurred after the death of Lenin and after Stalin's accession to power. The innovations in this period, of course, were collectivization and industrialization and the role they played in the shaping of the Soviet *apparat* and style—in general, the formation of the Soviet system as it has existed for the past sixty years. By the mid-1920s the Soviet regime had stabilized its control over a re-created, albeit somewhat truncated, Russia. However, the country over which it reigned was backward and, compared with the Western entities against which the Bolsheviks compared their Russia, even more backward than when they had struck for power a decade earlier. Something had to be done to modernize quickly, and this something was to be collectivization and industrialization.

The Stalinist revolution of the late 1920s and early 1930s created a model for the accelerated growth of backward countries, a model that was not only followed by Stalin and his successors but also was imposed on, or adopted (wholly or in part), by dozens of other countries on five continents.

Once Stalin had established his system, he made no major changes in it during the remaining decades of his life, though he did periodically indulge in cosmetic touchups and play at musical chairs with institutions and responsibilities. Some observers might consider the great purges of the mid-1930s and late 1930s as innovational, since those purges served as a vehicle for eliminating not only opposition, but even all potential sources of opposition, for creating opportunities for upward mobility, and for reducing the general population to apathetic compliance. The purges did effect significant societal changes, but it is highly questionable as to whether all those changes were intended. Moreover, terror and purges had not been unknown in the Soviet experience before the mid-1930s. If there was anything innovational about the great purges, it was their scope.

The second Soviet innovative period came under Nikita Sergeevich Khrushchev (1957-1962). By the time he took over, certain problems in Stalin's Soviet model were apparent. The model seemed to work well, given its objectives, in early stages of development, when economic apparatus was uncomplicated and the range of alternatives limited. But as the Soviet economy developed, centralized economic decision making did not work well, principally because of the burden it placed on the central apparatus and because of the lack of technical expertise at upper levels. As complexity increased and technology developed, the range of possible alternatives increased. In the 1920s, for example, there was no question that a strong steel industry was basic. But by the 1950s the question was posed as to whether steel should continue to receive the lion's share of investment capital or whether other metallurgical industries should not be pushed—if need be, even at steel's expense. In addition, the dysfunctionality of basing an advanced economic system on a terrorized and impoverished populace became apparent. In order the achieve continued industrial development, was it not necessary to restrain the secret police and raise the standard of living? Khrushchev had to decide whether to continue with the Stalin model or to innovate. He opted for the latter.

Though there have only been these two major innovational episodes in Soviet history—in the first of which Stalin established the Soviet system and in the second of which Khrushchev attempted to modify it—it is possible to identify some characteristics common to both periods.

First, both occurred immediately after a power struggle had come to an end but before the victor had succeeded in consolidating his power. In 1927, Stalin and, in 1957, Khrushchev had emerged victorious in the struggle for succession, but the opposition was not yet silenced. Moreover, even among those who had supported the winners, many were less than totally committed. Some had chosen Stalin or Khrushchev only as the least among several evils. The newly triumphant, aware that they had been practically nobody's first choice, felt called upon to prove themselves and to cement their political positions. And both attempted to do so by, among other things, innovating, by putting into effect changes that they themselves had by no means originated but that, in the course of the struggle for power, they had come to regard as necessary. Both proceeded to identify themselves with these changes.

A second characteristic common to both innovational periods is that they were dominated by individuals. Though neither Stalin nor Khrushchev possessed absolute power at the time, they nevertheless had sufficient control to institute their innovations. Among other high party members, there was insufficient opposition or show of opposition to head Stalin and Khrushchev off and prevent them from introducing their proposals.

Soviet patterns of innovation were distinctly limited, but it seems reasonable to speculate that innovation is more likely to occur in the Soviet system when a single individual is in charge than when collegial leadership prevails. When no single individual is head of the system, when there are a number of chiefs present in the Politburo (whether any of them covets the top power or not), factions develop. When one faction proposes changes, others are wary and hang back. Even when changes are effected in such a milieu, it is likely that they come about as the result of compromise and political deals. Under such circumstances, the possibilities for significant innovation are restricted—and that is precisely what happened to innovation in the post-Khrushchev era.

As to why the innovative periods were limited in duration, even Mao had to recognize that all innovative episodes cannot go on forever and are likely to be followed by periods of adjustment. Why were they nonrepetitive? In Khrushchev's case he simply was not around to try again. As for Stalin, there are several reasons why, in the twenty years after the First Five-Year Plan, he never again trod the path of innovation. First, collectivization, industrialization, and the purges—all of which he had introduced—brought about tremendous dislocations in the Soviet Union. Indeed, the country was only beginning to settle down when Hitler invaded. World War II was seen as no time for innovation, and the huge rebuilding effort after the war inhibited innovation in the Soviet Union as elsewhere. Then, by the time a bond of readjustment to peace had been achieved—though this was still in the midst of the Cold War—Stalin was over seventy and too set in his ways to attempt much that was new. But even if Stalin had had an earlier opportunity to innovate again, the evidence would seem to indicate that in industrialization, collectivization, centralization, and strict control—in the Soviet model—he had found the "way," and he would not have been prone to depart substantially from it.

Stalin, though perhaps bureaucratically imaginative, was not really an innovative personality. He did not particularly like the new and the different. They made him feel uncomfortable. He did not relish or value originality. (As he remarked on more than one occasion, it is not important *who* thinks of an idea, but *when* it is put into effect.) Once Stalin had found what he regarded as a winning combination—it had built the Soviet Union up, brought it victory over Hitler, made it one of the mightiest powers in the world, and kept him in power—he was not tempted to move very far away from it.

On the other hand, Khrushchev, unlike Stalin, was unmistakably interested in the new, a proclivity he maintained even out of power until the end of his years. But toward the closing of his tenure, it became clear that most of his innovations had failed or had met with less than overwhelming success and that his style as well as his lack of success had made his colleagues more and more reluctant to go along with his ideas. Here again it is to be observed that innovation does not require that the single leader have all power in his hands before he can innovate, but he must be in such a strong position that very few, if any, will attempt to interfere. When more than a few (particularly the most influential members of the PB) begin to have doubts that they are willing to express, even if only among themselves, then the leader is in trouble, and his potential for innovating is restricted. In the early 1930s, when there were doubters in the upper echelons, Stalin physically eliminated them. But by the time that Khrushchev's turn came, a psychological restraint against the use of terror had developed. He could not do what Stalin had done to the opposition, even had he so wished. In the early 1960s Khrushchev could, in most instances, still apparently have those he opposed at the *obkom* level removed from office, but he could not oust his opponents in the PB and their clients.

When Khrushchev had upset too many by his crudeness and insensitivity; as his innovations stepped on more and more toes and produced no outstanding successes; as his leadership in foreign affairs became suspect; and he developed no sizable corps of upwardly mobile supporters as Stalin had done; as his style shamed hundreds personally and seemed to embarrass the nation, Nikita Sergeevich found fewer and fewer willing to support or abide him. A PB cabal was organized against him—and he fell.

As Khrushchev had sought to deal with the problems of the Soviet system and with the problems of consolidating his own personal support, he had taken the position that there was nothing fundamentally wrong with the system; it required only a bit of fixing up. A nail had to be hammered more firmly here, a bolt tightened there. In practice, however, Khrushchev's changes—for example, the splitting of responsibility in the party secretariat, the decision to reduce the armed forces by one-third, the cutback in military production, the stepped-up emphasis on consumer industries, the instituting of limited decentralization—may have represented considerably more than tinkering. But, whether they did or not, they affected a great many important personages, often negatively as far as their own power positions were concerned. They thus turned these personages not only against Khrushchev, but determinedly against innovation ("harebrained schemes," they called them after

Khrushchev was ousted), with which Khrushchev had become identified as well.

Brezhnev, Khrushchev's successor as the first secretary of the party, understood, consciously or unconsciously, what seemed to be the lessons of the Khrushchev experience with respect to innovation. If you don't have the power to make it stick, and if you don't want to lose out, don't try it. If you are weak, and if your proposals don't work, the failure will be held against you and may lead to your removal, as it did to Khrushchev.

Brezhnev's colleagues at the head of the regime—Kosygin, Suslov, Podgorny, later Kirilenko, and their entourages—were tired of hassle. They had survived the terrors and anxieties of Stalin; they had been through the turmoil of the struggle for power that followed his death, the elimination of Beria and Malenkov, of Molotov and Kaganovich; they had been kept on edge seemingly constantly by Khrushchev. Now they were at the top. They wanted to stay there during the twilight of their lives, and they wanted things to be quiet.

At this stage, none of these survivors had the overwhelming compulsion to risk all to take power in his own right. Certainly Stalin had been determined to dominate. He was seemingly driven to do so from his youth. Khrushchev was less so. For Khrushchev, activity, movement, and involvement were more important than absolute power. It can be argued that Khrushchev would never have taken power in his own right if the opportunity for doing so had not fallen into his lap and if he had not been afraid of the consequences of not taking advantage of the opportunity. But it seems from what we know that Brezhnev never had the opportunity to take over in the same sense that Khrushchev had done. If he had moved to do so, his allies would have quickly turned to enemies. They had had enough of the "cult of the individual," regardless of who the individual was. They were content not to be "first," so long as no one was "first" over them.

Brezhnev was aware of the disposition of his associates and of his own weakness. He handled his colleagues in the PB—and the country—accordingly. He avoided making waves, he did not embarrass colleagues or countrymen, and he was dignified, avuncular, the soul of consideration. He took pains to see that a wide circle of those involved in matters at hand were consulted. Not only decisions, but the execution of decisions, more than ever before in Soviet history, were made with group awareness and involvement. There were few "personal" interpretations of what the PB had meant, as in Khrushchev's time. Brezhnev and company appeared content to let things and people continue as they had evolved. The continuity between the delegates elected to Twenty-Fourth Party Congress (1971) and Twenty-Fifth Party Congress (1976) is astounding. Eighty-nine percent of those elected in 1971 were reelected five years later. Not only were those at the top not about to change policies, they were not about to change personnel. They did not want to be ousted, and they were not about to threaten stability by ousting anyone else—unless someone began making difficulties, as for example, Shelepin and Podgorny seem to have done.

This affinity for the status quo does not indicate that the PB was not aware of difficulties developing in the system. PB members had improved informational channels and increasing amounts of accurate information, in spite of a persistent reluctance by those below to pass bad news up the line. The continuing and accelerating shortcomings of Soviet industry and agriculture were apparent. It was no secret in the PB that the rate of industrial growth had declined and seemed certain to go lower; nor was it a secret that there was increasing restiveness in the bloc countries, and even at home, and that "Eurocommunism" posed a potentially lethal threat. But to take the steps necessary to cope with such problems on more than a day-to-day basis, to make the changes necessary, was seemingly beyond the will and desire of the PB.

Those at the top of the Soviet system in the 1970s were reluctant to change because of advanced age—in 1977 all the top PB members were over seventy (and the average age in the CC was over sixty)—as well as because of the habits of a lifetime. These were men who had, for the most part, come up the hard way. They had developed with the Soviet system and were loyal to it. They had succeeded and survived, as they saw it, by being resolute. When faced with challenges, their inclination was not to give way before the demands of altered circumstance, but to tough it out. That, they told themselves, is how they had gotten where they were.

But most of all, Soviet leaders feared what innovation would bring. The continuation of development in the USSR, they saw, required decentralization and a reallocation of social and economic priorities on a wide scale. But such changes would certainly give rise to shifts in attitudes and controllability that could not but alter the entire Soviet universe and their positions in it. Decentralization and modified values implied reduction in their own authority and the participation of far wider circles in the decision making process—which was not acceptable to them. The PB of the post-Khrushchev, and particularly the post-Czechoslovak invasion period, responded to demands for change in three principal ways: by a "crackdown" against any attempt to change the status quo; by in effect permitting decisions implementing usually rather limited decentralization to be made *elsewhere* when it seemed absolutely impossible to avoid decentralization; and by détente.

As has been frequently pointed out, a strong impetus for détente on the Soviet side was the hope that the import of Western technology (which détente would facilitate) would overcome the shortcomings of Soviet technology and enable the regime to avoid the wholesale modifications it feared. (The social changes that the introduction of such technology might bring, though not unforeseen, were nevertheless played down. Their effect was not likely to be felt immediately.) Through détente, Soviet technology could be advanced. But the system would remain unchanged and the authority of the central leadership undisturbed.

But détente did not provide enough technology to bring the Soviet industrial apparatus up to Western standards. Soviet industry and technology not only continued to lag, but in some respects fell further behind the West. The Soviet leadership had no new remedies to offer. Their answer to the need for innovation was more of what they had been doing: stonewalling; giving in reluctantly, minimally, when they were convinced they could not avoid it; and continuing to latch on to détente and the hopes it held out.

In spite of the failure of the post-Khrushchev leadership to introduce innovations into the system, there is no reason in the late 1970s to believe that the system is about to topple. Certainly, it is not threatened by opposition forces with developed organizations and detailed plans for innovation. But it is threatened by the natural forces—of age, infirmity, and death. It is only a matter of time before several PB leaders will drop out. When Brezhnev passes on, if not the other top leaders, it is likely, though not certain, that a power struggle will ensue. In that case, if past experience holds true, innovation will be one of the major focuses of the debate around which the succession will be fought out. And the succession will quite likely lead to innovation as it did in the past, particularly if the struggle for power produces a single victor, who then, by implementing innovation, seeks to prove himself. It is not impossible that the passing of the top leaders will not lead to a power struggle. Perhaps Brezhnev, Suslov, and the others have agreed among themselves as to the succession. As each of them is no longer able to continue, he will perhaps be replaced by someone whom he had selected earlier from among his retinue. To guarantee stability, so as not to set a succession crisis in motion, the others will see that such a succession will be carried out.

Under those circumstances, it seems likely that the potential for innovation will be substantially less than if there were to be a struggle for power, a struggle from which a single leader would emerge.

In conclusion, innovation—thus far in the Soviet experience—has resulted when a power struggle has ended with one man in substantial, but by no means complete, control. That man has sought to build his reputation and personal machine by introducing new measures to deal with real problems. There is no reason why collective leadership cannot also innovate, but it is far more difficult to get a number of strong-willed individuals to agree as to whether there is a problem, how bad it is, and what ought to be done about it, than it is for a single man to formulate and take action. If, in the short run, there is to be significant, extensive innovation in the USSR, it seems reasonable to expect it to come most likely from a single individual who has become predominant in the Politburo.

List of Contributors

Arpad Abonyi is a doctoral candidate at Carleton University and the author of several papers on East European politics and economic development.

Gary K. Bertsch is Professor of Political Science at the University of Georgia. He is the author of a major textbook on comparative communist systems and a prolific author of articles on communism, in particular on Yugoslavia.

Richard V. Burks is Professor of History at Wayne State University. He is the author and editor of a number of works on Eastern Europe, including *The Future of Communism in Europe* and *Communist States in Eastern Europe.*

Andrew Gyorgy is Professor of International Affairs and Political Science at the Institute for Sino-Soviet Studies of The George Washington University. He has written and edited several books. He is Chairman of the Five-University Research Colloquium on the Soviet Union and Eastern Europe (Washington, D.C.) and a regular lecturer at the Foreign Service Institute of the U.S. Department of State, the National War College, and the Industrial College of the Armed Forces.

Martin O. Heisler is Associate Professor of Government at the University of Maryland, the editor of *Politics in Europe,* and the author of numerous articles on Western European politics.

Dan N. Jacobs is Professor of Government at the University of Miami and the author of numerous books on Soviet and world communism.

Roger E. Kanet is Associate Professor of Political Science at the University of Illinois. He has written widely in the field of comparative politics and Soviet and East European government.

James A. Kuhlman is Associate Professor of Government and International Relations at the University of South Carolina, and the author and editor of books on Eastern European integration, military power, strategies and alliances, and issues related to the global strategic balance.

Peter C. Ludz is Professor of Political Science at the University of Munich, the author of major books on East German politics, and a specialist on the Soviet Union and Eastern Europe.

John M. Starrels is Assistant Professor of Political Science at The George Washington University, coauthor of a major book on East German politics, and the author of several articles on East–West European relations.

Joan Barth Urban is Associate Professor of Politics at the Catholic University of America. A specialist in Italian politics, she has written widely on Western Europe and Eurocommunism.

List of Contributors

William A. Welsh is Professor of Political Science at the University of Iowa and Director of the Laboratory for Political Research at that university. He is the author of several books on comparative politics as well as numerous articles on political and social development.

Robert S. Wood is Associate Professor of Government in the Woodrow Wilson School of Foreign Affairs of the University of Virginia. In 1977-78 he was Visiting Professor at the U.S. Naval War College in Newport, Rhode Island.

Index

The following abbreviations have been used throughout this index:

CDU	Christian Democratic Union
COMECON	Council for Mutual Economic Assistance
CPSU	USSR Communist Party
CSCE	Conference on European Security and Cooperation
CSU	Christian Socialist Union
DC	Christian Democrats
EEC	European Economic Community, Common Market
GDR	German Democratic Republic, East Germany
GFR	German Federal Republic, West Germany
LCY	League of Communists
PCE	Spanish Communist Party
PCF	French Communist Party
PCI	Italian Communist Party
PCP	Portuguese Communist Party
PS	Socialist Party of France
SED	Socialist Unity Party (GDR)
SPD	Social Democratic Party

Abonyi, Arpad, 8
Adams, John Quincy, 160
Albania, 101
Allende, Salvatore, 127
Alliance of the Left (Union de Gauche), 187-188. *See also* PCF
Amalrik, Andrei, 69
Andreotti, Giulio, 118. *See also* Christian Democrats
Arbatov, Georgi, 184
Argentina, 144
Aron, Raymond, 191
Asia, 75

215

Atlantic Alliance, 180
Atlantic Charter, 148
Austria, 79, 133

Bahr, Egon, 105
Balkans, 100
Basic Treaty of 1973 (GDR), 105, 111, 112
Bauman, Zygmunt, 41
Baylis, Thomas, 48
Belgrade, 100, 113
Beria, Lavrenti, 206
Berlin Conference. See Conference of European Communist and Workers' Parties
Berlin Wall, 111
Berliner, Joseph S., 3
Berlinguer, Enrico, 66, 108-109, 118, 185, 187. See also PCI
Bernstein, Eduard, 108
Bertsch, Gary K., 7
Bologna, 63
Bolsheviks, 145, 200, 201
Bonn, 107
Brandt, Willy, 105, 108
Brazil, 144
Brezhnev, Leonid, 104, 130, 196
  "Brezhnev doctrine," 152
  and France, 120, 188
  and leadership, 206-207, 209
  and peaceful coexistence, 153
Britain, 145
Brzezinski, Zbigniew, 184, 185, 191
Budapest, 194
Bulgaria, 28, 32
  Academy of Science, 21
  and Eurocommunism, 126, 133, 138, 190
  science in, 25, 34-37
Burks, R. V., 3, 92

Carrillo, Santiago
  and CPSU, 129, 131, 137, 184-185, 187

and Eurocommunism, 67-68, 107-109, 192
Carter, Jimmy
  foreign policy, 143
  human rights campaign, 144, 149-151, 153, 158-160, 179, 184
Catalonia, 67
Center-Right (France), 66
Central Europe, 100
Central planning, 28
Cervetti, Gianni, 125
Charter 77. See Czechoslovakia
Chile, 127
China, 196
  and CPSU, 120, 130
  post-Mao leadership, 93
  and Yugoslavia, 83-84, 91
Christian Democratic Union (CDU), 109. See also GFR
Christian Democrats (DC). See also Italy
  "historic compromise," 60, 128
  intra-party agreement, 71
  and PCI, 63-64, 69-70, 118
Christian Socialist Union (CSU), 109
Club of Rome, 191
Cold War, 155, 204
Cominform, 77, 80, 179
Comintern, 133, 179, 200
Committee for Social Self-Defense (KOR). See Poland
Common Market. See European Economic Community
Conference of European Communist and Workers' Parties (East Berlin, 1976), 115, 129-132, 195
  Eastern Europe, 109, 132, 137
  Eurocommunism and, 117, 130, 132, 181
Conference on European Security and Cooperation (CSCE). See Helsinki Conference

Index

Council for Mutual Economic Assistance (COMECON), 78-80, 87, 169
Croan, Melvin, 42
Croatia, 99, 100-102, 104
Cunhal, Alvaro, 118. See also PCP
Czechoslovakia, 45-47, 101, 104, 171-174. See also Prague
  Charter 77, 52, 133, 135
  dissidents, 53, 115
  and Eurocommunism, 126, 138, 190-191
  invasion of (1968), 117, 118
  and PCI, 135-136
  reform movement, 49
  reforms in, 48, 88-92, 164
  and USSR, 121, 127, 208
  and Yugoslavia, 84, 87

Carrillo, Santiago
  and CPSU, 129, 131, 137, 184-185, 187
  and Eurocommunism, 67-68, 107-109, 192
Carter, Jimmy
  foreign policy, 143
  human rights campaign, 144, 149-151, 153, 158-160, 179, 184
Catalonia, 67
Center-Right (France), 66
Central Europe, 100
Central planning, 28
Cervetti, Gianni, 125
Charter 77. See Czechoslovakia
Chile, 127
China, 196
  and CPSU, 120, 130
  post-Mao leadership, 93
  and Yugoslavia, 83-84, 91
Christian Democrats (DC). See also Italy
  "historic compromise," 60, 128
  intra-party agreement, 71
  and PCI, 63-64, 69-70, 118

Christian Democratic Union (CDU), 109.
Christian Socialist Union (CSU), 109
Club of Rome, 191
Cold War, 155, 204
Cominform, 77, 80, 179
Comintern, 133, 179, 200
Committee for Social Self-Defense (KOR). See Poland
Common Market. See European Economic Community
Conference of European Communist and Workers' Parties (East Berlin, 1976), 115, 129-132, 195
  Eastern Europe, 109, 132, 137
  Eurocommunism and, 117, 130, 132, 181
Conference on European Security and Cooperation (CSCE). See Helsinki Conference
Council for Mutual Economic Assistance (COMECON), 78-80, 87, 169
Croan, Melvin, 42
Croatia, 99, 100-102, 104
Cunhal, Alvaro, 118. See also PCP
Czechoslovakia, 45-47, 101, 104, 171, 174. See also Prague
  Charter 77, 52, 133, 135
  dissidents, 53, 115
  and Eurocommunism, 126, 138, 190-191
  invasion of (1968), 117, 118
  and PCI, 135-136
  reform movement, 49
  reforms in, 48, 88-92, 164
  and USSR, 121, 127, 208
  and Yugoslavia, 84, 87

Danube, 100
"Dictatorship of the Proletariat," 60, 187-188

Djilas, Milovan, 26, 77
Doonesbury, 151
Dubček, Alexander, 127
Dubrovnik, 83

East Berlin, 194
East Berlin Conference (1976). *See* Conference of European Communist and Workers' Parties
Eastern Europe, 43-47, 53, 93, 100, 107, 122, 185
  Berlin Conference (1976), 109, 132, 137
  change in, 26-27, 29, 41, 86
  communist parties in, 190. *See also specific countries*
  decision making in, 32
  economic planning in, 17
  and Eurocommunism, 59-61, 70, 113, 115, 121, 125, 137-138, 179-196
  Helsinki Conference, 110
  and human rights, 151, 153
  innovation in, 163, 170-171, 174, 177
  scientists in, 24, 27, 30, 35-37
  and self-management, 91
  and Soviet influence, 165-169
  and Yugoslavia, 84-85, 90, 95
Ethiopia, 144
Eurocommunism, 59-70, 115-140, 179-196
  Berlin Conference (1976), 117, 130, 132, 181
  and CPSU, 130, 179-180
  in Eastern Europe, 125-126, 133, 137-138, 179-196
  in France, 65, 66, 132, 186
  in Germany, 105-109, 113
  in Italy, 65, 68, 186
  in Spain, 68, 186
  and USSR, 207
  in Yugoslavia, 186, 190
Europe, 59, 62, 64, 83, 148
  intra-German relations, 113
  and Soviet scholars, 124
  state system, 153-154
European Economic Community (EEC, Common Market), 62, 100

Fascism, 106
Filov, Bogdan, 22
Fleron, Frederick J., Jr., 31
France, 67, 145. *See also* PCF, PS, Paris
  Eastern Europe and, 190
  elections (1978), 71
  Eurocommunism in, 65-66, 68-70, 115, 183, 186
  Gaullists, 65-66
  presidential race (1974), 129
  and USSR, 189
Franco, 66-67, 128-129
French Communist Party (PCF), 122. *See also* Marchais, Georges
  Berlin Conference (1976), 109
  "common program," 60, 66, 119
  and CPSU, 59, 128, 130, 132
  electoral support of, 62
  and Eurocommunism, 117, 182
  and PCE, 120
  and PCI, 120
  and PS, 65, 68
  Twenty-First PCF Congress (1974), 119
  Twenty-Second PCF Congress (1976), 119
  and USSR, 180, 184-187, 189
French Revolution, 154
Fromm, Erich, 191
Fulbright, J. William, 148

Galtung, Johan, 167
Gati, Charles, 195
Gdańsk riots, *See* Poland

Index

George Washington University, 2
German Democratic Republic (East Germany, GDR), 30, 79, 171-172. *See also* SED
  change in, 45, 86, 174
  dissidents and, 133
  New Economic System, 48, 88
  and Eurocommunism, 105-109, 190-191
  human rights and, 110-112
  intra-German relations, 105-114. *See also* Basic Treaty of 1973
  reform in, 164, 173
  self-management in, 91, 94
  "Third Way" doctrine, 106
  and USSR, 90
German Federal Republic (West Germany, GFR), 133. *See also* SPD, CDU, CSU
  Bundeswehr, 189
  and Eurocommunism, 105-109
  and intra-German relations, 105-114
Germany, 145, 166
Geshov, Ivan, 22
Gierek, Edward, 126, 134-137
Gitelman, Zvi, 41, 87, 93
Gonzales, Felipe, 67
Graham, Loren, 21
Granick, David, 79
Greece, 184
Griffith, William E., 184
Griffiths, Franklyn, 42, 44

Havemann, Robert, 125
Heisler, Martin O., 6
Helsinki agreements, 53, 131, 179
Helsinki Conference, 110, 111, 113
"Historic compromise." *See* DC, PCI
Hitler, Adolf, 203, 204
Honecker, Erich, 108
Human rights, 110, 112, 143-144.
  See also Carter, Jimmy
Hungary, 20, 45, 79, 101
  New Economic Mechanism (NEM) (1968), 49, 172-174
  and Eurocommunism, 126, 133, 138, 180, 190, 195
  policy science in, 28, 34-36
  reform movement, 49
  reforms in, 86-88, 164
  and USSR, 90-92, 94
  and Yugoslavia, 83
Huntington, Samuel P., 191

International Institute for Applied Systems Analysis (IIASA), 35
Internationalist solidarity, 123
Italian Communist Party (PCI), 62-66, 108-109, 114, 185-187
  and DC, 69
  and CPSU, 59, 124-126, 130, 137, 184
  and Eurocommunism, 117-120, 122, 132, 182, 191
  "historic compromise," 60, 128
  intra-party agreement, 71
  and Poland, 135-136, 138
  and USSR, 180
Italy, 79, 100, 133, 190. *See also* PCI, DC
  divorce referendum (1974), 129
  and Eurocommunism, 63, 115, 183, 186
  intra-party agreement, 71
  PCI in, 66, 69-70, 135

Jacobs, Dan N., 9
Janos, Andrew, 42, 43, 44, 47
Japan, 156

Kádár, János, 126, 133
Kaganovich, Lazar M., 206
Kanet, Roger E., 67, 87
Kardelj, Edward, 103

Kennan, George F., 145-147, 160
Kennedy, John F., 143
Khrushchev, Nikita Sergeevich, 23, 201-209
  and Yugoslavia, 84, 89
Kirilenko, A. P., 206
Kissinger, Henry, 143, 145, 151, 156-159
Kissinger-Sonnenfeld doctrine, 61
Korbonski, Andrzej, 41, 42
Kosovo, 101, 102
Kosygin, Alexei N., 106
Krakow, 134, 135
Kremlin, 129, 146-147, 186. See also USSR
Kupa River, 100
Kuron, Jacek, 133

Lane, David, 42, 50
League of Communists (LCY), 87
  and CPSU, 190
  leadership role, 78, 80, 94-95, 99-104
Left Radical Movement, 65-66, 119
Lenin, Vladimir I. Ulyanov, 76, 77, 108, 200. See also Marxism-Leninism
Leninism, 103, 182
Libermanism, 48
Lincoln, Abraham, 150
Lipinski, Edward, 133
Lippman, Walter, 148
Lister, Enrique, 184
Lodge, Milton, 31
Ludz, Peter C., 8

Macedonia, 101
Madrid, 120, 181
Malenkov, Georgi, 206
Maoism, 196
Mao Tse-tung, 203
Marchais, Georges, 66, 108
  and CPSU, 132, 185, 187-188
  and Eurocommunism, 119-120
Marcuse, Herbert, 191
Marshall Plan, 155
Marx, Karl, 148
Marxism, 51, 94, 151-153
  industrial democracy, 76-77
  and self-management, 80
Marxism-Leninism, 45, 106-109, 173-174, 191
  in Eastern Europe, 113-114, 163, 165, 168-171, 177
  and Eurocommunism, 60, 182, 186
Marxism-Leninism-Stalinism, 103
  and science, 21
  in USSR, 190, 193
Medvedev, Roy, 125
Merleau-Ponty, Maurice, 191
Meyer, Alfred G., 191
Mitterrand, François, 65, 119, 187-188. See also PS
Modernization, 44
Mlynar, Zdenek, 133
Molotov, Vyacheslav, 206
Montenegro, 104
Moscow, 67, 92, 123-130, 196. See also USSR
  and Eastern Europe, 169
  and Eurocommunism, 138
  and human rights, 184
  and PCF, 188
  and PCI, 137
  Twenty-fifth CPSU Congress, 132
The Movement for the Defense of Human and Civil Rights, 51. See also Poland

Napoleon, 154, 155
Naroll, Raoul, 18
National Socialism, 106
North Atlantic Treaty Organization (NATO), 62, 135, 180, 189

Index

Paris, 83, 181
Peking, 118, 120
Pluralism, 103, 111, 127
 and Eastern Europe, 44
 and Eurocommunism, 116-117
 and Yugoslavia, 101
Podgorny, N. V., 206, 207
Poland, 20, 45-46, 94, 171. *See also* Gierek, Edward
 dissidents in, 53, 115, 126, 133-136
 and Eurocommunism, 138, 180, 190, 193, 195
 Gdańsk riots (1970), 49-50
 The Movement for the Defense of Human and Civil Rights, 51
 Politburo, 48
 science in, 34-35
 and USSR, 90-92
 Workers' Defense Committee (KOR, Committee for Social Self-Defense), 46, 50-52, 133-135, 137
 and Yugoslavia, 83-84
Politburo (PB). *See* USSR and CPSU
Polycentrism, 183
Ponomarev, Boris, 124
"Popular Front," 66
Portugal, 129
Portuguese Communist Party (PCP), 117-118, 128, 132. *See also* Cunhal, Alvaro
 and USSR, 121, 196
Prague, 118, 124, 127, 194

Radice, Lucio Lombardo, 125
Radio Free Europe, 144, 193
Radio Liberty, 144, 193
Red Army, 148
Red Square, 147
Reformation, 154
Regionalism 116-118, 129, 184
Reston, James, 160
Roman Catholic Church, 45, 51, 154
Rome, 181
Rubbi, Antonio, 136
Rumania, 79, 123, 131, 171
 and CPSU, 132
 and Eurocommunism, 130, 190, 193, 195

Sartre, Jean-Paul, 191
Sava River, 100
Schaff, Adam, 26
Selucky, Radoslav, 173
Serbia, 104
Sharp, Samuel, 89, 90
Shelepin, Alexander N., 207
Sigur, Dr. Gaston J., 9
Sik, Endre, 172
Skilling, H. Gordon, 42
Slovenia, 45, 102, 104
Sobolev, Alekander, 124
Social Democratic Party (SPD), 107, 108, 185
Socialist Alliance (Yugoslavia), 102
Socialist Party of France (PS), 70. *See also* Mitterrand, François
 common program, 60, 66, 119
 and PCF, 65, 68, 187, 189
Socialist Unity Party (SED), 191
 and Eurocommunism, 107-110, 113-114, 125
 and human rights, 110-112
Socialist Workers' Party (Spain), 67, 68, 70. *See also* Gonzales, Felipe
Sofia, 101
South Korea, 144
Soviet Union. *See* USSR
Spain, 62, 66, 129. *See also* PCE, Socialist Workers' Party
 Eurocommunism in, 68, 69, 115, 186, 191
 first elections (1977), 67

and Eurocommunism, 117-120, 122
and PCF, 132
and USSR, 186
Spanish Communist Party, 117-118, 120, 122, 128
and CPSU, 129, 132, 184, 186-187
and Eurocommunism, 67-68
Stalin, 42, 43, 53
control of society, 46
on fascism and social democracy, 185
"popular front" concept, 183
post-Stalin, 47
purges, 205, 206
Soviet model, 200-204
and Yugoslavia, 190
Stalinism, 79, 93
and PCF, 182
in USSR and East Europe, 121-122
Starrels, John M., 7
State Department, 143-144
Strategic Arms Limitation Talks (SALT), 113
Suarez, Adolfo, 67
Suslov, Mikhail, 124, 125, 206, 209
Sweden, 184
Szczepanski, Jan, 47

Teilhard de Chardin, Pierre, 191
Third Reich, 106
Third World, 144, 153, 167, 170
Thirty Years' War, 154
Timofeev, Timur, 124
Tito, Josip Broz, 77, 99
and China, 83-84
and Croatian Republic, 104
Treaty of Westphalia, 153, 155, 158
Trotsky, Leon, 26
Truman Doctrine, 155

Ulbricht, Walter, 108
Union of the Left (France), 119, 120
Union of Soviet Socialist Republics (USSR), 131, 145-148, *See also* CPSU; Brezhnev, Leonid; Kremlin
Carter and, 151
and Chile, 127
communism in, 114
decision making, 23
détente (peaceful coexistence), 152-153
dissidents, 144
and East Germany (GDR), 106-107
and Eastern Europe, 20, 27, 60-61, 116-167, 169, 172, 175-177, 192
economic planning in, 17-18
and Eurocommunism, 59, 68, 70, 108, 115-117, 120, 138, 179, 183-186, 193-196
and Europe, 124
human rights, 184
intervention in Czechoslovakia, 48, 118
interventions, 91
leadership in, 93-94
and PCE, 67, 128, 180
and PCF, 65, 119, 132, 188-189
and PCI, 124-125, 135-136, 180
policy science in, 28-37
Politburo, 199-200, 203-205, 207-210
and proletarian internationalism, 133
resistance to change, 26
science in, 21, 24-25
Sino-Soviet dispute, 120
Soviet bloc, 110, 126
Soviet-U.S. foreign policy, 155-160
on Western revolution, 130

Index

and Yugoslavia, 75, 77, 80, 83-84, 86-95, 190
USSR Communist Party (CPSU), 123-131, 199
  and Eastern Europe, 169
  and Eurocommunism, 59, 179-181, 183, 185-186, 190, 192, 195-196
  and PCF, 65, 187-189
  and PCI, 137
  Politburo, 124, 189, 199-200
  Twenty-Fifth Party Congress (1976), 207
  Twenty-Fourth Party Congress (1971), 132, 207
United Nations, 149
United States, 61
  détente, 152, 156
  and human rights campaign, 144, 149-151, 159-160
  organizational democracy in, 79
  U.S.-Soviet foreign policy, 145-149, 157-160, 184
  and Western Europe, 155-156
Uruguay, 144
Urban, Joan Barth, 8
Urbanization, 45

Vietnam, 155
Voice of America, 193

Warsaw, 134, 136, 137, 194
Warsaw Pact, 117-118, 131
Welsh, William A., 5, 67
West, 60, 123, 138, 191. *See also* Western Europe
  East-West relations, 61, 127, 129
  Eurocommunism and, 181, 183, 186, 193
  industrialism and the Third World, 167
  interventions against the USSR, 145
  liberal democracies, 43-44
  revolution in, 126
  technology, 175-176, 208
  view of Berlin Conference (1976), 115
  Western trade credits, 53
West Berlin, 111
Western Alliance, 61
Western Europe, 26, 115, 122. *See also* West Berlin Conference (1976), 132
  communist parties in, 106-107, 128-129, 194
  and Eastern Europe, 101, 166
  Eurocommunism in, 59-62, 68, 70, 179-180, 185-186
  and GDR, 144
  socialism in, 113
  and USSR, 196
  U.S. and, 155-156
White House, 144
Winthrop, John, 150
Wood, Robert S., 8
Workers' councils, 78, 86, 87
Workers' Defense Committee (KOR). *See* Poland
Workshop Conference on the Adoption and Diffusion of New Ideas within the Socialist Community (April 29-30, 1977), 2
World Bank, 81
World Conference of Communist and Workers' Parties, 127
World War II, 106, 108, 111, 163
  pre-World War II Eastern Europe, 45-46
  and USSR, 204
  U.S. foreign policy since, 156

Yalta Declaration, 148
Yugoslavia, 20, 35, 123, 138, 180.

See also Tito, Josip Broz; LCY
and CPSU, 130, 132, 190
Croatian crisis (1971), 99
elections, 102
and Eurocommunism, 186, 190, 193, 195
First and Second International Conferences on Participation and Self-Management (1972, 1977), 83
influence on Eastern Europe, 86-89, 92
innovations in, 76
People's Army, 104
Pluralization of, 100
Politburo, 77
self-management, 76-97
Socialist Alliance, 102

Zagladin, Vadim, 124, 131
Zarodov, Konstantin, 124, 126, 133, 136
Zhivkov, Todor, 133

Augsburg College
George Sverdrup Library
Minneapolis, Minnesota 55454